Computer Accounting
Essentials
with
QuickBooks® 2012

Computer Accounting Essentials with QuickBooks® 2012

Versions Pro, Premier & Accountant

Sixth Edition

Carol Yacht, MA
Software Consultant

Susan V. Crosson, MS, CPA
Emory University

McGraw-Hill
Irwin

McGraw-Hill
Irwin

COMPUTER ACCOUNTING ESSENTIALS WITH QUICKBOOKS® 2012, SIXTH EDITION

Published by McGraw-Hill/Irwin, a business unit of The McGraw-Hill Companies, Inc., 1221 Avenue of the Americas, New York, NY 10020. Copyright © 2013, 2011, 2009, 2007, 2005, 2002 by The McGraw-Hill Companies, Inc. All rights reserved. Printed in the United States of America.

1 2 3 4 5 6 7 8 9 0 RMN/RMN 1 0 9 8 7 6 5 4 3 2
ISBN-13: 978-0-07-802557-0
ISBN-10: 0-07-802557-5

Publisher: *Tim Vertovec*
Executive editor: *Steve Schuetz*
Editorial coordinator: *Danielle Andries*
Senior project manager: *Diane L. Nowaczyk*
Senior buyer: *Michael R. McCormick*
Senior design coordinator: *Joanne Mennemeier*
Marketing manager: *Dean Karampelas*
Media project manager: *Alpana Jolly, Hurix Systems Pvt. Ltd.*

www.mhhe.com

About the Authors

Carol Yacht is a textbook author and accounting educator. Carol is the author of Peachtree, QuickBooks, Microsoft Dynamics-GP, and Excel textbooks, and the accounting textbook supplement, Carol Yacht's General Ledger and Peachtree DVDs (www.mhhe.com/yacht). Carol taught on the faculties of California State University-Los Angeles, West Los Angeles College, Yavapai College, and Beverly Hills High School. To help students master accounting principles, procedures, and business processes, Carol includes accounting software in her classes.

An early user of accounting software, Carol Yacht started teaching computerized accounting in 1980. Yacht's teaching career includes first and second year accounting courses, accounting information systems, and computer accounting. Since 1989, Yacht's textbooks have been published by McGraw-Hill.

Carol contributes regularly to professional journals and is the Accounting Section Editor for *Business Education Forum*, a publication of the National Business Education Association. She is also the Editor of the American Accounting Association's Teaching, Learning, and Curriculum section's *The Accounting Educator*.

Carol Yacht was an officer of AAA's Two-Year College section and recipient of its Lifetime Achievement Award. She is a board member of the Microsoft Dynamics Academic Alliance, worked for IBM Corporation as an education instruction specialist, served on the AAA Commons Editorial Board, NBEA's Computer Education Task Force, and works for Intuit as an education consultant. She is a frequent speaker at state, regional, and national conventions.

Carol earned her MA degree from California State University-Los Angeles, BS degree from the University of New Mexico, and AS degree from Temple University.

Susan V. Crosson teaches at Emory University. Previously she was a Professor and Coordinator of Accounting at Santa Fe College in Gainesville, FL. She has also taught on the faculties of University of Florida, Washington University in St. Louis, University of Oklahoma, Johnson County Community College, and Kansas City Kansas Community College. Susan is known for her innovative application of pedagogical strategies online and in the classroom. She likes to speak and write on the effective use of technology throughout the accounting curriculum. Susan is co-author of several accounting textbooks including the Computer Accounting Essentials series.

Susan served as a Supply Chain Leader on the AAA and AICPA sponsored Commission on Accounting Higher Education: Pathways to a Profession. She also serves on the Relations with Accounting Educators Committee and the Financial Literacy Committee for the Florida Institute of CPAs. She is the incoming President of the Teaching Learning and Curriculum Section of the American Accounting Association (AAA). Previously she served AAA as Chair of the Conference on Teaching and Learning in Accounting, a Vice President of Sections and Regions, Chair of the Membership Committee, Council Member-at-large, and Chair of the Two-Year Accounting Section. For the AICPA she has served on the Pre-certification Education Executive Committee.

In 2010, Susan received AAA's Outstanding Service Award. Previously, she has received the Outstanding Educator Award and Lifetime Achievement Award from the American Accounting Association's Two Year College Section, the Florida Association of Community Colleges Professor of the Year Award for Instructional Excellence, and University of Oklahoma's Halliburton Education Award for Excellence.

Susan earned her Master of Science in Accounting from Texas Tech University and her undergraduate degree in accounting and economics from Southern Methodist University. She is a CPA.

Preface

Computer Accounting Essentials with QuickBooks 2012 teaches you how to use QuickBooks software (QB 2012). QuickBooks 2012 is a financial management program created for small businesses.

Read Me: QuickBooks Online, QuickBooks for Mac, QuickBooks Pro, QuickBooks Premier, or QuickBooks Enterprise Solutions

Depending on the business, Intuit publishes a QuickBooks product to meet its needs. QuickBooks Online is a web-based accounting solution. The other QuickBooks products are desktop solutions for businesses of varying complexity ranging from QuickBooks for Mac, QuickBooks Pro, QuickBooks Premier, or QuickBooks Enterprise Solutions. QuickBooks also tailors its Premier and Enterprise products to industry needs—accounting professionals, contractors, manufacturers, nonprofits, professional services, retailers, wholesalers, and distributors. For more information about the various QuickBooks products, go online to http://quickbooks.intuit.com.

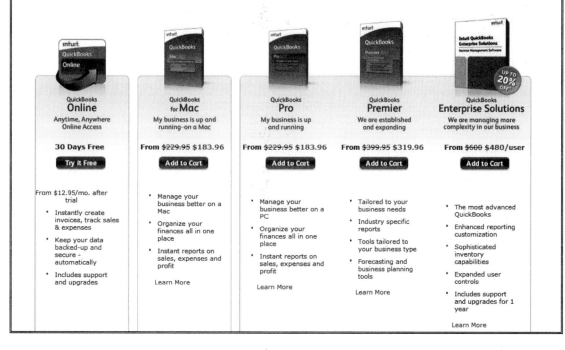

QB 2012 is a comprehensive accounting program that includes sales order and purchase order processing, banking, inventory management, and payroll. You can also share information with Office programs, such as Word, Excel, and Outlook.

 Read me: Student software CD included with textbook _and_ classroom site licenses.

For Students:
The software included with the textbook is accessible for a single user for 140 days. Students can work both at school and on their personal computers using external media, such as an USB drive, to backup and transport their files between locations.

For Classrooms:
For software installation in the school's computer lab or classroom, please refer to the Intuit Education Program at www.Intuitaccountants.com/educationyacht; link to Educational Products; or email education@intuit.com.

As of this writing, the cost for QuickBooks 2012 Accountant for Windows classroom site licenses is:

o   10 Pack $300.00*
o   25 Pack $460.00
o   50 Pack $690.00
*Pricing is subject to change.

QuickBooks Accountant 2012 includes access to other QB versions with the toggle feature.

Additional resources are available on the Online Learning Center (OLC) at www.mhhe.com/QBessentials2012. The OLC includes chapter resources, including troubleshooting tips, online quizzes, etc.

QUICKBOOKS 2012

Each textbook includes a 140 day single-user copy of the QuickBooks Accountant 2012 Student Trial Edition software for students to install and use on their individual computers.

Computer Accounting Essentials with QuickBooks 2012 shows you how to set up and operate a merchandising business. When you complete the textbook you will have a working familiarity with QuickBooks software.

TEXTBOOK ORGANIZATION BY CHAPTER

1: Software Installation and Creating a New Company

After verifying your computer meets or exceeds the system requirements, you install QB 2012. Following the Express Start Interview you create a new company and then back it up. Finally, using the Learning Center Tutorials, the videos provide instruction about the tasks and workflows shown on the Home page.

2: Exploring QuickBooks

There are many sample companies included with the software. You explore a sample product company and a sample service company to learn about QB 2012's user interface, internal controls, and help resources. In addition, you review user roles, customize the privileges of a user, and e-mail a company backup to your professor.

3: New Company Setup for a Merchandising Business

In this chapter, you begin operating a retail business called Your Name Retailers Inc. You enter beginning balances for October 1 of the current year, edit the chart of accounts, record and post bank transactions, complete bank reconciliation, and print reports. Detailed steps and numerous screen illustrations help you learn how to use QB 2012.

4: Working with Inventory, Vendors, and Customers

In this chapter you complete two months of transactions for a retail business to learn basic business processes. You set up vendor preferences, defaults and inventory items, record vendor transactions, make vendor payments, record sales transactions, and collect customer payments. You also complete bank reconciliation, display various reports, and prepare financial statements.

5: Accounting Cycle and Year End

In this chapter you review the accounting cycle and complete end-of-year adjusting entries, print financial statements, and close the fiscal year.

6: First Month of the New Year

In this chapter you begin the new fiscal year, record one month of transactions for your business, make adjusting entries, and print reports.

Project 1: Your Name Hardware Store is a comprehensive project that incorporates what you have learned in Chapters 1-6. In Project 1, you analyze typical source documents used by a merchandising business and complete the accounting cycle.

Project 2: Student-Designed Merchandising Business asks you to create a merchandising business from scratch.

Appendix A: Review of Accounting Principles. Appendix A is a review of basic accounting principles and procedures.

Appendix B: Troubleshooting and QuickBooks Tips. Refer to this window for additional troubleshooting tips.

Appendix C: Glossary. Appendix C is a glossary of terms.

Index: The textbook ends with an index.

SAVING QUICKBOOKS 2012 DATA FILES

QuickBooks can store your data several different ways. In this text, you save or backup work using either QuickBooks backup files (.QBB extensions) or QuickBooks portable company files (.QBM extensions).

Local backup: .QBB

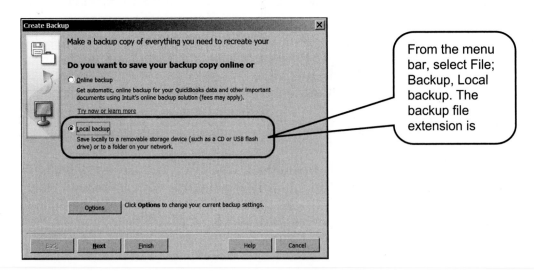

From the menu bar, select File; Backup, Local backup. The backup file extension is

Portable company file: .QBM

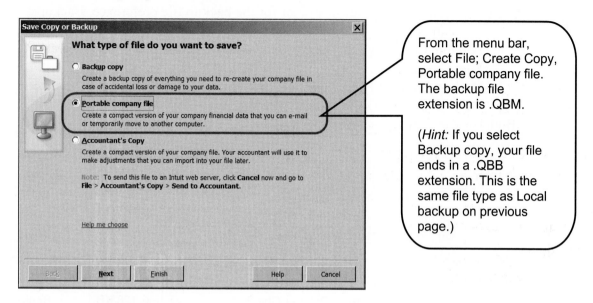

From the menu bar, select File; Create Copy, Portable company file. The backup file extension is .QBM.

(*Hint:* If you select Backup copy, your file ends in a .QBB extension. This is the same file type as Local backup on previous page.)

CONVENTIONS USED IN TEXTBOOK

As you work through the chapters, read and follow the step-by-step instructions. Numerous screen illustrations help you check work.

1. Information that you type appears in **boldface**; for example, Type **Melody Harmony** in the Customer name field.

2. Keys on the keyboard that are pressed appear like this: <Tab>; <Enter>.

3. Unnamed buttons and icons are shown as they appear on the window; for example, , Refresh , etc.

4. Read Me boxes go into more detail about the task you are completing. Whenever you see a Read Me box, review this information.

5. Footnotes provide information about the task you are completing.

Refer to the chart on the next page for chapter, backup file names, file sizes and page numbers where files were backed up.

> **Read Me: Backup Preference**
>   Check with your instructor for the backup file preference. Backups can be made a couple of ways.
> 1. Portable Company Files (.QBM extension): From the menu bar, select File; Create Copy.
> 2. Backup Copy (.QBM extension): From the menu bar, *either* File; Create Backup; or File; Create Copy, Backup Copy.
>
> Both backup files types are shown in the text.

Chapter	Backups (.QBB and .QBM extensions)	File Size*	Page No.
1	Your Name Retailers Inc.QBB	5,952 KB	18-20
	Your Name Hardware Store.QBB	6,400 KB	26
2	sample_product-based business.QBM	1,616 KB	31-33
	Your Name Chapter 2 End.QBM	1,619 KB	55
	Your Name sample_service-based business.QBM	1,100 KB	62
3	Your Name Chapter 3 October 1.QBB	6,072 KB	77
	Your Name Chapter 3 October Check Register.QBB	6,128 KB	87-88
	Your Name Chapter 3 October End.QBB	6,196 KB	101
4	Your Name Chapter 4 Vendors and Inventory.QBB	6,268 KB	120
	Your Name Chapter 4 Vendors.QBB	6,332 KB	134
	Your Name Chapter 4 November.QBB	6,480 KB	155
	Your Name Chapter 4 End.QBB	6,592 KB	165-166
	Your Name Exercise 4-2 December.QBB	6,720 KB	172
5	Your Name Chapter 5 December UTB.QBB	6,800 KB	181
	Your Name Chapter 5 December Financial Statements.QBB	6,816 KB	188
	Your Name Chapter 5 EOY (Portable).QBM	643 KB	192
6	Your Name Chapter 6 January Check Register.QBB	6,880 KB	205
	Your Name Chapter 6 UTB.QBB	6,980 KB	209
	Your Name Chapter 6 January Financial Statements.QBB	7,052 KB	212
	Your Name Exercise 6-1 (Portable).QBM	743 KB	217
Project 1	Your Name Hardware Store Beginning Balances (Portable).QBM	337 KB	224
	Your Name Hardware Store Vendors Inventory Customers (Portable).QBM	343 KB	228
	Your Name Hardware Store January (Portable).QBM	353 KB	239
	Your Name Hardware Store Complete (Portable).QBM	441 KB	241

*File sizes may differ.

Table of Contents

Comment:
The Timetable for Completion is meant as a guideline for hands-on work. Work can be completed in class or as a standalone outside of class project.

TIMETABLE FOR COMPLETION		Hours
Chapter 1	Software Installation and Creating a New Company	1.0
Chapter 2	Exploring QuickBooks	1.0
Chapter 3	New Company Setup for a Merchandising Business	2.0
Chapter 4	Working With Inventory, Vendors, and Customers	3.0
Chapter 5	Accounting Cycle and Year End	2.0
Chapter 6	First Month of the New Year	1.0
Project 1*	Your Name Hardware Store	3.0
Project 2	Student-Designed Merchandising Business	3.0
TOTAL HOURS:		**16.0**

*Project 1 is the culminating project in the text. Typical source documents are used for transaction analysis, including accounts payable, inventory, accounts receivable, cash, and bank reconciliation. The accounting cycle is completed for one month. An audit trail report is also completed.

Computer Accounting
Essentials
with
QuickBooks® 2012

Chapter 1

Software Installation and Creating a New Company

OBJECTIVES:

1. System Requirements.
2. Software Installation.
3. Starting QuickBooks.
4. Creating a New Company.
5. Registering QuickBooks.
6. Backing up Company Data.
7. QuickBooks Learning Center.

IMPORTANT MESSAGE: QuickBooks 2012 Student Trial Edition

QuickBooks 2012 Student Trial Edition will operate for 140 days **after** registering your installation on a single computer. After installation, you only have <u>30 days</u> to register. **If you fail to register, after 30 days your software will stop working.**

The Student Trial Edition has limited use and cannot be networked in computer labs. Schools must purchase and install QuickBooks 2012 licenses for their computer labs. (Refer to the Preface, page viii, For Students; For Classrooms.)

SYSTEM REQUIREMENTS

These are the system requirements for QuickBooks 2012. QuickBooks Accountant 2012 is the software packaged with the textbook.

- Windows XP (SP3), Vista (SP1 inc 64-bit), or 7 (inc 64-bit)

- At least 2.0 GHz processor (2.4 GHz recommended)

- 1GB of RAM for a single user

- Minimum 2.5 GB of available disk space (additional space required for data files)

- 250 MB for Microsoft .NET 4.0 Runtime, provided on the QuickBooks CD

- Minimum 1024 X 768 screen resolution, 16-bit or higher color

- 4x CD-ROM

- All online features/services require Internet access (fees may apply).

- Product registration required

- High-speed Internet connection (DSL, cable modem, or higher)

- Internet Explorer 6 or higher must be installed on every computer running QuickBooks.

- Microsoft Word® and Excel® 2003, 2007, or 2010 (inc 64-bit).

- External media for backups: One 2 GB or higher **USB drive**. See the Part openers for backup files sizes. The default location for backing up is C:\Users\Public\Public Documents\ Intuit\ QuickBooks\Company Files. You may also specify a hard-drive or external media location for backups.

Actual requirements and product functionality may vary based on the system configuration and operating system. For complete requirements, visit http://quickbooks.intuit.com. Third-party services are available for additional fees.

SOFTWARE INSTALLATION

This section gives you instructions for installing QuickBooks 2012 software on a single computer. (Instructions for uninstalling QuickBooks are included in Appendix B, pages 266-268.)

The QuickBooks Accountant 2012 Student Trial Edition installation steps are consistent with Windows 7. If you are using a different operating system, your steps may differ slightly.

Step 1: Turn on your computer. Close all programs and sign off the Internet. *QuickBooks works best if you are not connected to the Internet.* Microsoft Outlook should *not* be open. If Microsoft Outlook or any Virus protection programs are open, close them, along with other programs that may be open.

Step 2: Insert the QuickBooks 2012 Student Trial Edition Limited Use Only CD into the CD drive.

Step 3:   Click Run setup.exe. When the User Account Control window appears, click <Yes>. (If Setup does *not* start, open Windows Explorer and double-click the QuickBooks icon.) Be patient, it will take a few minutes for the installer to start.

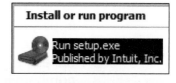

Step 4:   The Welcome to QuickBooks window appears. Click Next >.

Step 5:   The License Agreement window appears. After reading the terms of the Software License Agreement, print it for your files and select "I accept the terms in the license agreement." Click Next >.

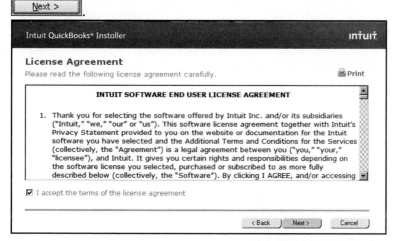

Step 6:   For Installation type, select "Express (recommended)." Click Next >.

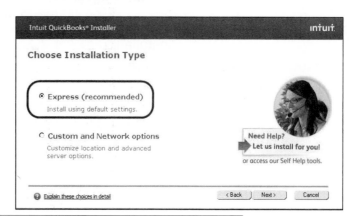

Step 7: When the License Number and Product Number window appears, enter your license number and product number. These can be found on the Intuit label attached to the CD envelope which is included with the text. (Keep your installation numbers in a safe place. You will need them if you reinstall your QuickBooks software.)

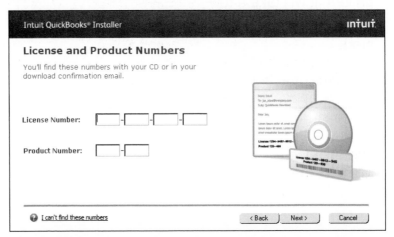

Step 8: Proofread your License and Product numbers, then click Next >.

Step 9: When the Ready to install window appears with the License and Product numbers shown, print a copy for your records. Click Install.

Step 10: An Installation in progress window appears. This process may take up to 20 minutes. Read the information while QuickBooks copies installation files. Note: If any Firewall or Security pop-up windows occur during setup, select Always Allow.

Step 11: A QuickBooks Installation Complete window appears. Click Finish.

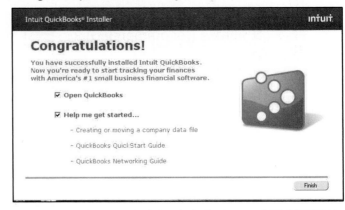

If an Internet Explorer window appears that say "Active content can harm your computer….read this information. The Don't show this message again box should be checked. Click <Yes>.

Step 12:   A window appears listing your options about how to get started with QuickBooks.

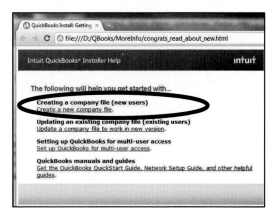

Step 13:   Select "Creating a new company file (new users)" by clicking on the link. (If you are online, you may get directed to the QuickBooks Support website. Close your Internet browser. The QuickBooks Express Start window appears.

Step 14:   Click on "Express Start."

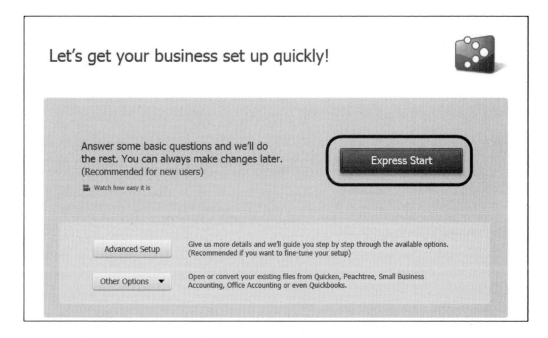

Step 15: In the next section, you will create a company by completing the QuickBooks Setup windows similar to the one shown here.

Tell us about your business

Enter the essentials so we can create a company file that's just right for your business.

Tell us ── Contact info ── Add info → Start working

* Company Name	
	We'll use this on your invoices and reports, and to name your company file.

* Industry Construction   Help me choose

We'll use this to create accounts common for your industry.

* Company Type ▼   Help me choose

We'll use this to select the right tax settings for your business.

Tax ID # EIN: 12-3456789 or SSN: 123-45-6789

We'll use this on your tax forms.

* Required

Need help? Give us a call   Back   Continue

Step 16: Open your CD drive and remove the QuickBooks 2012 CD.

CREATING A NEW COMPANY

Follow these steps to create a new company in QuickBooks 2012.

1. The "Tell us about your business" window is displayed.

2. Complete the Company Name field, **Your Name Retailers Inc.** (use your first and last name), e.g., Carol Yacht Retailers Inc.

3. For Industry, click on "Help me choose." The Select Your Industry window appears. Scroll down list and highlight "Retail Shop or Online Commerce." Compare your window to one shown here. Click `OK`.

4. For Company Type, click on the pulldown arrow and then select "Corporation."

5. Leave Tax ID # Blank.

6. Compare your entries to the window shown here, when satisfied, select `Continue`.

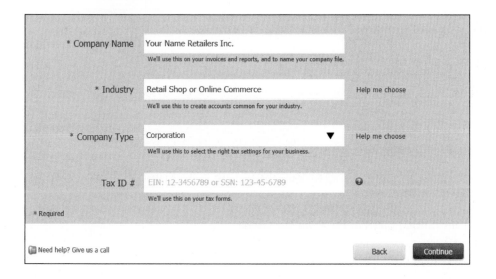

7. The Enter your business contact information window appears. Complete it using your contact information.

Legal name: **Your Name Retailers Inc.** (use your first and last name)
Street: **Your address**
City: **Reno**
State: **Nevada**
Zip: **89557**
Country: U.S.
Phone: **Your phone number**
E-Mail: **Your e-mail**
Web site: **leave blank**

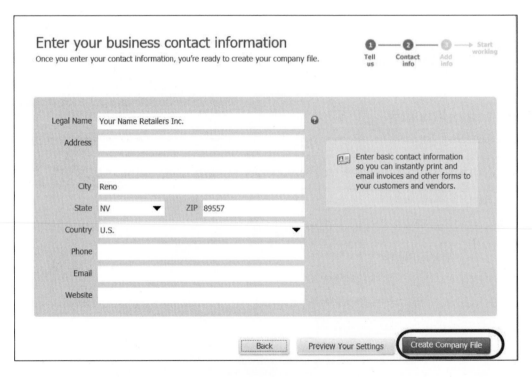

Your address, phone, and email should be completed.

When satisfied, click [Create Company File].

8. Wait while QuickBooks creates the new company file.

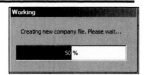

9. When the "You've got a company file!" window appears, select "Add your bank accounts" by clicking on [Add].

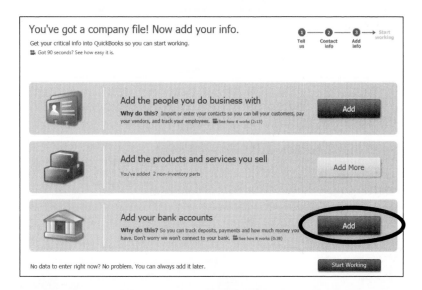

10. On the "Add your bank accounts" window, type **Home State Bank** for the account name. Then click [Continue].

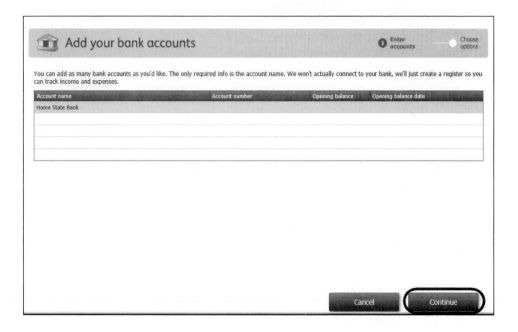

11. Select "No Thanks" to ordering checks from Intuit. Click 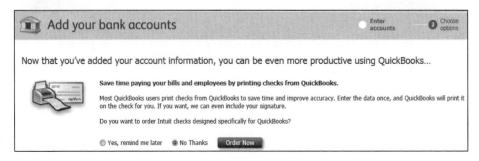.

12. The "You've got a company file!" window reappears. Since you will add the people you do business with and the products and services you sell later, select [Start Working].

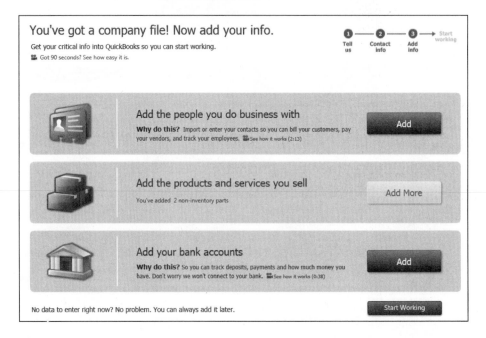

13. If a Ready to Start working? window appears, close it by clicking <X> on its title bar.

14. The Your Name Retailers Inc. desktop appears. If any other pop ups occur, return to your desktop.

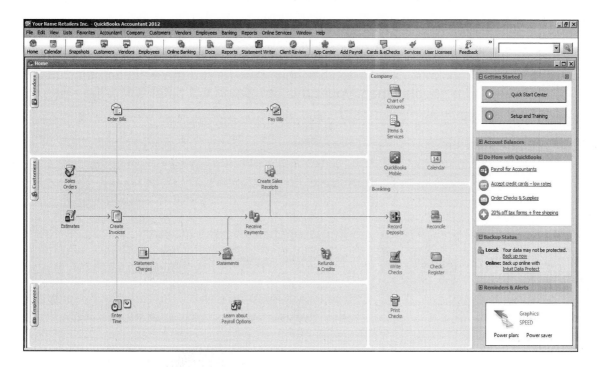

REGISTERING QUICKBOOKS

To use QuickBooks more than 30 days, you must register with Intuit.
Follow these steps to register your account with QuickBooks.

1. From the QuickBooks Desktop, select Help; Register QuickBooks.

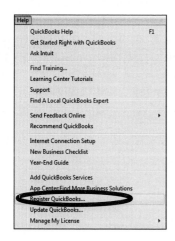

2. The "Register QuickBooks Now" window appears stating how many days remain before you will be locked out of the program. To avoid the lockout, pick **Register**. (If you have already started QB a couple times, your days remaining will differ. Click the <Begin Registration> button.)

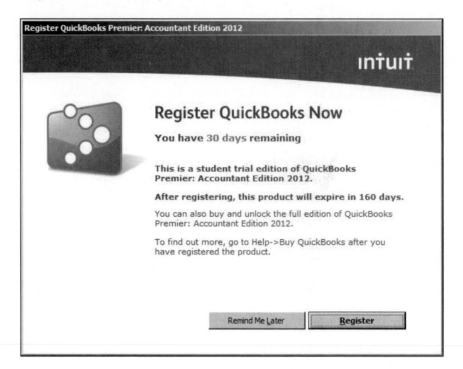

3. The Contacting QuickBooks window appears, checking to see if you are able to register online.

4. To complete registration, you will need to provide the following information.

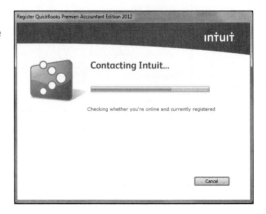

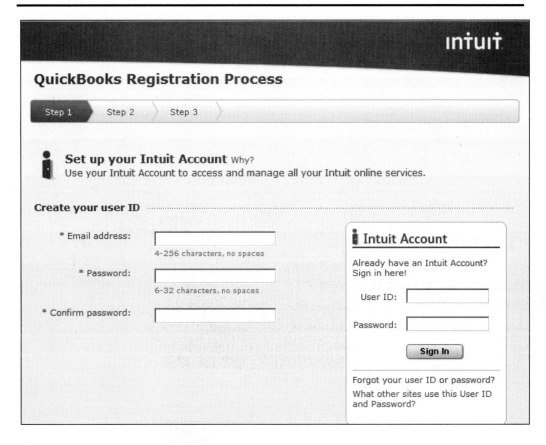

Your security word will differ.

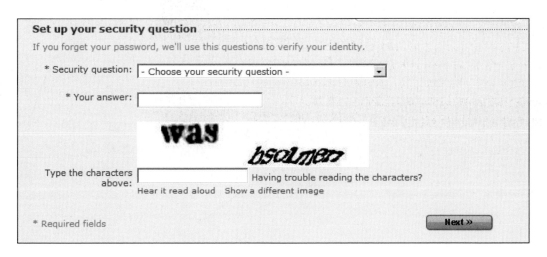

Review your business profile

[Clear All Fields]

Company information

* Country: `United States` ▾

* Company name: `Your Name Retailers Inc.`

* Industry: `Retail Shop or Online Commer` ▾

* Address 1: `Your address`

Address 2: `[            ]`

* City: `Reno`

* State: `NV` ▾

* Zip / Postal code: `89557`

* Business phone: `[   ] [   ] [   ]`

> Type the name of your company [i.e., Your first and last name Retailers Inc.] and the required fields will automatically fill.
>
> Type your address and phone number.

Primary contact

* First name: `[            ]`

* Last name: `[            ]`

Job title: `- Select Job Title -` ▾

* Primary phone: `[   ] [        ]` ext. `[`

Alternate phone: `[   ] [        ]`

* Email address: `[            ]`

> Type your first and last name, a job title, your phone number, and the email you used to create this account.

TRUSTe CERTIFIED PRIVACY   **A confirmation email will be sent to this address.**

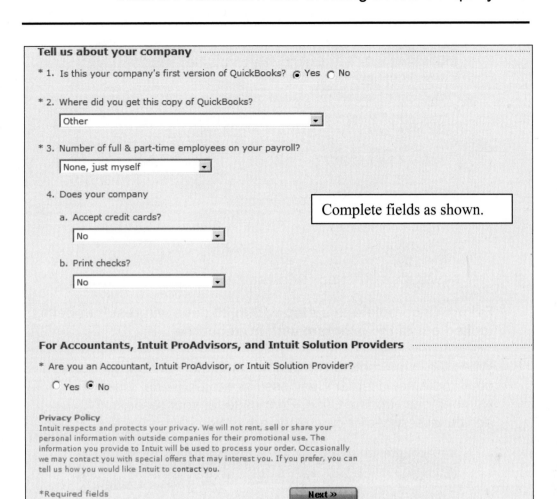

5. You can either call Intuit on the telephone or complete registration process over the web without a QuickBooks expert. Select "on the web" and click **Next »**.

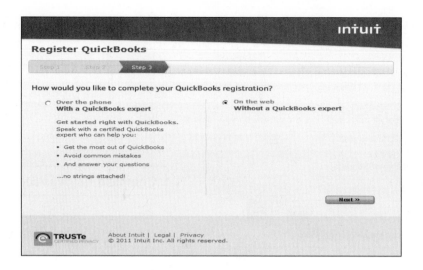

Failure to complete this step within 30 days will result in being locked out of the program with no recourse.

6. When the "Your registration is now complete" window appears, confirm Name, User ID, Business Phone, Zip Code, License Number, and Product Code. Print page for your records. No additional services or purchases are required!

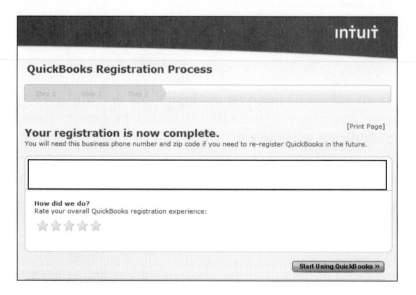

7. Select 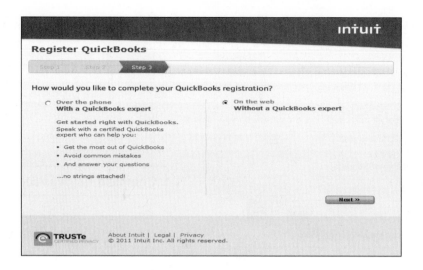 to return to your QuickBooks desktop.

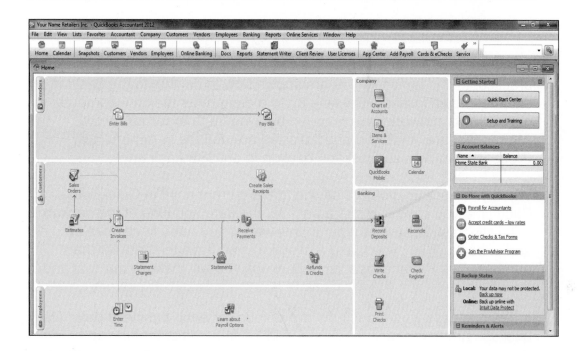

SOFTWARE REGISTRATION

If Register QuickBooks is available on the Help menu, you have not registered your copy of QuickBooks. You can verify that your copy of QuickBooks is registered by pressing the <F2> key when QuickBooks is open. The Product Information window appears and displays either REGISTERED or UNREGISTERED based on the registration status.

You can register QB by calling 800-316-1068 or 888-246-8848; or outside US, 520-901-3220. Once the software included with the textbook is registered, you have access for 140 days.

---

8.   To view your completed registration information for QuickBooks Accountant 2012, press the <F2> function key. **You have 140 days of use. After that time, the software is not accessible.** The Product Information window includes an Installed field that shows the date QB was installed. You have 140 days from the Installed date to use the student trial edition software included with this textbook.

BACKING UP COMPANY DATA

Frequent saving or backing up of company data is a good business practice. In this textbook, you are shown how to backup to the desktop or external media location. Backing up to a drive other than the computer's hard drive or network drive is called backing up to **external media**. (Words that are boldfaced and italicized are defined in Appendix C, Glossary.) Authors suggest you backup to an USB flash drive.

When you back up, you are saving to the current point in QuickBooks. Each time you save or make a backup, the date and time of the backup will distinguish between them. In this way, if you need to **restore** an earlier backup (i.e., you make a mistake), you have the data for that purpose. See Preface for a list of backups you will make in this text and their file size.

In the business world, backups are unique for each business day. Daily backups are necessary. If you are working in a computer lab, *never leave the computer lab without first backing up your data to external media, i.e., your USB flash drive.*

Saving to the Desktop or External Media
As a part of QuickBooks' attention to internal control and risk avoidance, the program will ask if you are certain that you want to back up company data to your desktop since the backup will reside in the same place as the actual data. Saving or backing up to external media such as a USB drive minimizes risk!

Follow these steps to save Your Name Retailers Inc. company data.

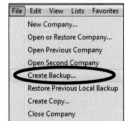

1. From the QuickBooks Desktop, click File; Create Backup.

2. Select Local backup. The local backup allows you to transport files on a USB drive or other external media to another computer (i.e. school's computer lab) or send it to your Accountant (your professor). Note that this is the first of many backups that you will make in this text as you operate your business. Click Next >.

---

3. The Backup Options window appears. Click [Browse...], then select your USB drive. Click [OK]. In the illustration, drive D:\ is shown. (Your drive letter may differ.) You can backup to a USB drive, other external media, or the desktop. Type **1** in the Remind me to back up when I close my company file. Click [OK].

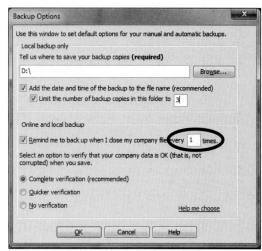

4. The When do you want to save your backup copy? window appears, select Save it now.   Click [Finish].

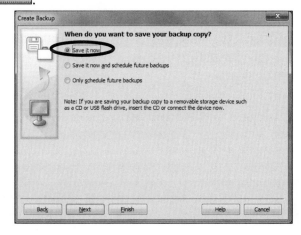

5. The Working window appears while your file is being backed up. When the backup is complete, a window such as the one shown below appears to confirm the date, time, and location of the saved company data. Click [OK].

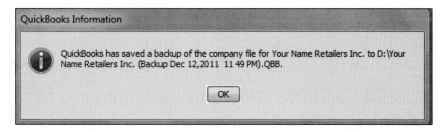

6. You are returned to the QuickBooks desktop, which is also called the Home page. The Backup Status area shows when you backed up.

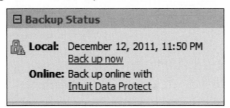

7. Exit program or continue working on the next section.

QUICKBOOKS LEARNING CENTER

QuickBooks has extensive learning resources, videos, and guides available as you learn the program. Let's take a look at how QuickBooks coaches you.

1. From the QuickBooks desktop, Select Quick Start Center from the Getting Started pane.

2. Review the various Get started on the right foot resources. To learn more about QB, select the Learning Center tutorials.

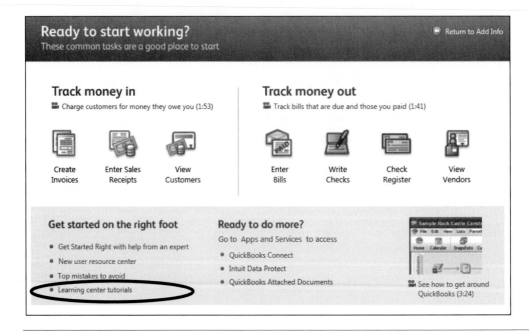

3. In the Overview & Setup section, select a video to learn how to set up the basics, for example, Overview of QuickBooks accounts. Close the window when you are ready to return to the QuickBooks desktop.

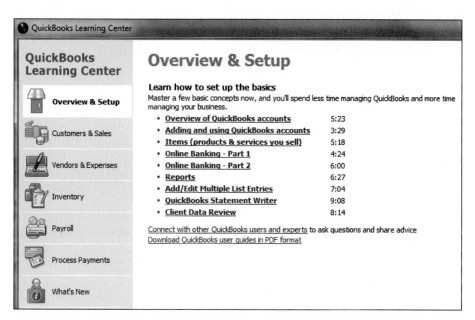

4. On the desktop, do not click on "Setup and Training" as it is a fee-based service.

5. Explore the Company, Customer, Vendor, and Banking workflow paths you will learn about in the following chapters, by clicking on the various icons on your company desktop.

6. Continue working on the next section or exit QuickBooks. To exit, select File; then click on Exit in the pull down menu or click on the **X** in upper right hand corner of your screen.

SUMMARY AND REVIEW

OBJECTIVES:

1. System Requirements.
2. Software Installation.
3. Starting QuickBooks.
4. Creating a New Company.
5. Registering QuickBooks.
6. Backing up Company Data.
7. QuickBooks Learning Center.

Additional textbook related resources are on the textbook website at www.mhhe.com/QBessentials2012. It includes chapter resources, online quizzes, etc.

RESOURCEFUL QUICKBOOKS

Go to the QuickBooks website http://quickbooks.intuit.com/. Explore it to answer the following questions.

1. Why use accounting software?

2. Why would I choose QuickBooks Accountant over QuickBooks Pro?

3. Click on the Support tab and then select Intuit Support for QuickBooks Desktop, list two popular topics.

4. Click on the New User Resource Center (within Intuit QuickBooks Support) and list two of the Top Mistakes to Avoid.

Multiple Choice Questions: The Online Learning Center includes the multiple-choice questions at www.mhhe.com/QBessentials2012, select Student Edition, Chapter 1, Multiple Choice.

_____1. QuickBooks Student Trial Edition will operate for how many days after registration?

    a. 30 days.
    b. 60 days.
    c. 120 days.
    d. 140 days.

_____2. Once QuickBooks Student Trial Edition is installed, which of the following icons will appear on the desktop:

    a. Support for QuickBooks.
    b. QuickBooks Library.
    c. QuickBooks 2012.
    d. Payroll for QuickBooks.

_____3. The Welcome to QuickBooks window allows users to:

    a. Explore QuickBooks.
    b. Open an existing company file.
    c. Create a new company.
    d. All of the above.

_____4. The name of the company created in Chapter 1 is:

    a. Your Name Retailers Inc.
    b. Your Name Merchandisers.
    c. Sample product-based business.
    d. Sample service-based business.

_____5. The type of business created in Chapter 1 is:

    a. Nonprofit.
    b. Repair and maintenance.
    c. Retail shop or online commerce.
    d. Sales-independent contractor.

_____6. The business created in Chapter 1 will operate as a:

    a. Sole proprietorship.
    b. Corporation.
    c. LLP.
    d. LLC.

_____7. The business created in Chapter 1 does:

    a. Accept credit cards.
    b. Print checks.
    c. Employ many employees.
    d. Accept cash and checks.

_____8. Software registration with Intuit must be completed within how many days of installation?

    a. 30 days.
    b. 60 days.
    c. 120 days.
    d. 140 days.

_____9. Account registration information can be viewed from the QuickBooks desktop by selecting which function key?

    a. <F1>.
    b. <F2>.
    c. <F3>.
    d. <F4>.

_____10. The cash balance at Home State Bank is:

    a. $0.
    b. $50,000.
    c. $80,000.
    d. $100,000.

True/Make True: To answer these questions, go online to www.mhhe.com/QBessentials2012, link to Student Edition, Chapter 1, QA Templates. The analysis question on the next page is also included.

1. QuickBooks Pro 2012 Student Trial Edition can only run on Vista computers.

2. QuickBooks 2012 Student Trial Edition can be installed on both individual and computer lab computers.

3. If QuickBooks is registered, the Help menu shows Register QuickBooks.

4. Creating a new company in QuickBooks is easy with the Express Start Interview.

5. You can close the application you are working with if you single click with your mouse on the close button ().

6. It is a good idea to regularly back up or save to the hard drive instead of external media such as a USB drive.

7. The new company that you created is a sole proprietorship.

8. The new company that you created accepts credit cards.

9. The new company that you created prints checks.

Exercise 1-1: Follow the instructions below to complete Exercise 1-1:

1. Start QuickBooks.

2. From the QuickBooks desktop, select File; click on New Company.

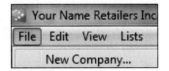

3. Use Express Start to create a corporation named **Your Name Hardware Store.** This is the business you will use to complete-Project 1. *HINT:* Use the Creating a New Company information on pages 6-11, steps 1-14, to set up Your Name Hardware Store.

4. Continue with Exercise 1-2.

Exercise 1-2

1. Back up. The suggested file name is **Your Name Hardware Store.QBB**. Detailed steps for backing up data are shown on pages 18-20, steps 1-7.

2. Exit QuickBooks 2012.

Analysis Questions:

1. How do you locate information about whether or not your software is registered?

2. How long do you have to register the software?

3. What is the time period for accessing the QuickBooks Accountant 2012 student trial edition software included with the textbook?

Chapter 2

Exploring QuickBooks

OBJECTIVES:

1. Start QuickBooks 2012 (QB).
2. Open the sample product-based business,
3. Backup and restore the sample business.
4. Overview of QuickBooks 2012.
5. QuickBooks Help, Preferences, and Product Information.
6. QuickBooks Internal Control features.
7. Using Windows Explorer.

Additional textbook related resources are on the textbook website at www.mhhe.com/QBessentials2012. It includes chapter resources, QA Templates, etc.

In Chapter 2, you become familiar with some of the QB features. There are two sample businesses included with the software: a product company and a service company. You explore the sample product business to learn about the QB user interface, internal controls, and help resources. In addition, you review procedures to backup and restore company data, use Windows Explorer, and e-mail a company backup to your professor.

GETTING STARTED

1. Start QuickBooks 2012 by double clicking on the QuickBooks icon on the computer desktop.

2. If you have not done so, register your student trial version (you have 30 days from installation to do this). You will need to be connected to the Internet to complete registration. If you are connected, click **Begin Registration**. Follow registration steps detailed in Chapter 1.

OPEN SAMPLE COMPANY

Sample company data files for a sample product-based business and a sample service-based business are included with the software. Follow the steps below to open starting data for the sample product-based company, Sample Rock Castle Construction. Similar steps can be followed to open data from the sample service-based company, Sample Larry's Landscaping and Garden Supply.

1.   From the QuickBooks 2012 desktop, select File; Close Company.

2.   A No Company Open window appears. Click on the link to <u>Open a sample file</u>.

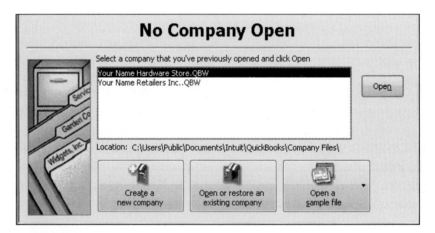

3.   Select Sample product-based business.

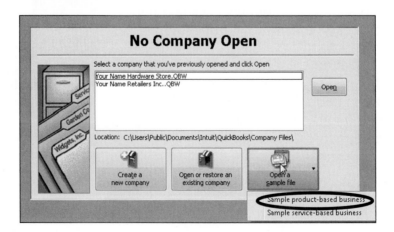

4. When the QuickBooks Information prompts "This is the QuickBooks sample file," read the information, then click [OK].

   A product based company purchases merchandise from vendors, and then sells that merchandise to customers. Products fall into two categories: inventory and non-inventory items. Another way to describe a product-based company is to call it a merchandising or retail business. The sample company that you are going to use, Sample Rock Castle Construction, is a product based business.

5. If a QuickBooks usage student window appears, click <No>. When the Accountant Center window appears, click <X> to close it. Then, click on the box next to Show Accountant Center when opening a company file to *uncheck* it. When the box is unchecked, the Accountant Center window will not show when you start QB. Then click on the title bar's [X], then [OK] to close the Accountant Center window.

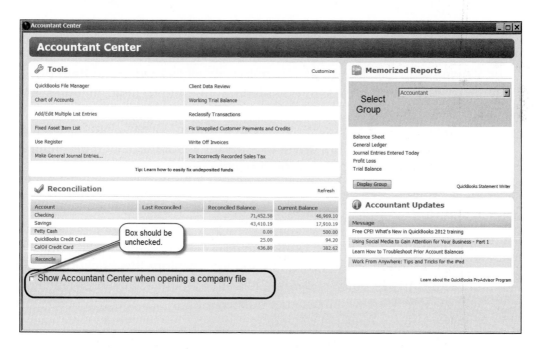

6. The Sample Rock Castle Construction – QuickBooks 2012 Home page appears. Compare yours with the one shown on the next page. The various parts of the QB Home page are explained later in the chapter.

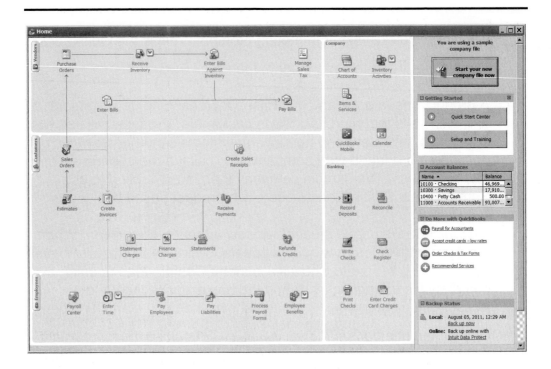

BACK UP AND RESTORE SAMPLE COMPANY

When using QB, information is automatically saved to the hard drive of the computer. In a classroom setting, a number of students may be using the same computer. This means that when you return to the computer lab or classroom, your data is gone. *Backing up* your data means saving it to a hard drive, network drive, or external media. Backing up ensures that you can start where you left off the last time you used QuickBooks 2012.

Back Up Sample Company

In this section you will create a backup of the original starting data for the sample product-based business and then restore this backup file. This backup is made *before* any data is added to the sample company so if you want to start with fresh, beginning data again, you can restore from this backup file of the original data.

Comment

In this textbook, you are shown how to backup to external media, i.e., an USB drive location. Backing up to a drive other than the hard drive or network drive is called backing up to external media. The instructions that follow assume you are backing up to external media. Authors recommend backing up to at least an **2 GB USB flash drive OR if you are working on your own computer, your desktop.**

When you back up, you are saving to the current point in QB. Each time you make a backup, you should type a different backup name (file name) to distinguish between them. In this way, if you need to restore an earlier backup, you have the data for that purpose. See Preface for a list of backups you will make in this text and their file size.

In the business world, backups are unique for each business day. Daily backups are necessary. If you are working in a computer lab, *never leave the computer lab without first backing up your data to external media, i.e., your USB flash drive.*

The text directions assume that you are backing up to *an external media* location. Follow these steps to back up QuickBooks 2012.

1. From the menu bar, select File; Create Copy.

2. The Save Copy or Backup window appears. Select Portable company file for the type of file you want to save and then click 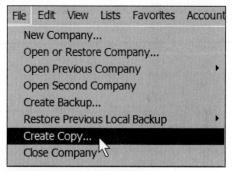.

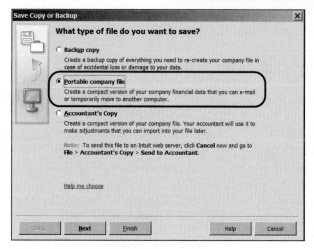

---

3. When the Save Portable Company window appears, go to your USB drive location and create a new folder titled, Your Name (your first and last name) QB Backups.

4. Click on Your Name QB Backups folder to open it. Notice the File name is sample_product-based business (Portable). Click

    Save .

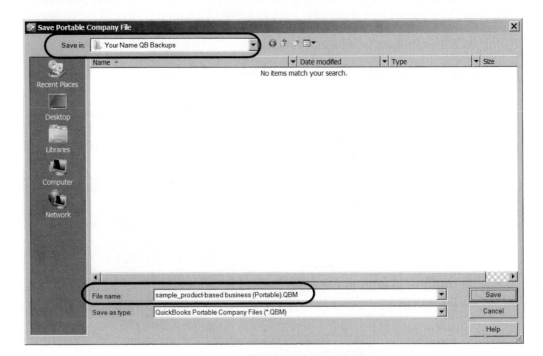

5. When Close and reopen window appears, click

    OK .

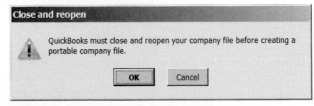

6. When the QuickBooks Information window appears, read and then

    click OK .

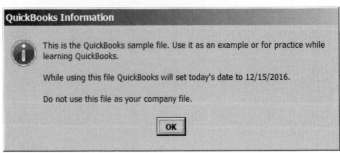

7. The Creating Portable Company File window appears while your data is being backed up. When the QuickBooks Information screen appears, click [OK].

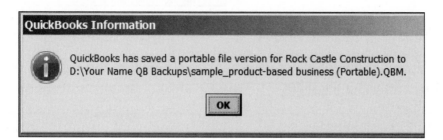

8. You are returned to Sample Rock Castle Construction - QuickBooks 2012. Close the Accountant Center window.

9. Click [X] on the title bar to exit Sample Rock Castle Construction or File; Exit and return to the windows desktop. (*Or, continue with the next section without exiting.*)

10. If you want to back up the starting data for Larry's Landscaping and Garden Supply (the sample service-based business) follow similar steps to create its backup file.

   Read me: Data Files

Refer to the Preface, to review information about the several types of QB files. The Preface also lists the names of all the backups you will make in this text.

Locate the Backup File

The steps that follow assume that the backup file was saved to external media. Follow these steps to locate the backup file.

1. Right click on [start] or [ ]. Then left click Open Windows Explorer (Windows 7) or Explore (Vista or XP). My Computer window appears.

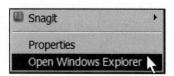

---

2. Select your USB drive. In this example PKBACK# 001 (D:).

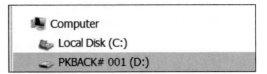

3. Double-click on the Your Name QB Backups folder to open it.

4. Observe the address of your backup file. This is the location of the file. File size may differ.

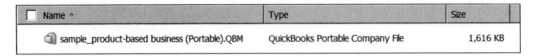

Name ^	Type	Size
sample_product-based business (Portable).QBM	QuickBooks Portable Company File	1,616 KB

Portable files automatically add a .QBM extension. If your file extension does <u>not</u> appear, do this:

a. From the Windows Explorer menu bar, select Organize, Folder and search options.

b. The Folder Options window appears. Click the View tab. Hide extensions for known file types should be *unchecked*.

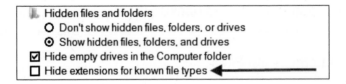

c. On the Folder Options window, click <OK>. Close Windows Explorer.

Restore Sample Company

1. Start QuickBooks 2012. (If necessary, select, Start; All Programs, QuickBooks, QuickBooks 2012.)

2. The QuickBooks 2012 desktop appears. Make sure Sample Rock Castle Construction - QuickBooks 2012 is open. (If not, select File; Open Previous Company, \sample_product-based business.qbw.)

   (*Hint:* When using QB, information windows may appear. For example, if a window prompts that the sample company is being used, click <OK>.)

Click File; Open or Restore
Company…

3. The Open or Restore Company window appears. Select Restore a
   portable file. Click ⟨ Next > ⟩.

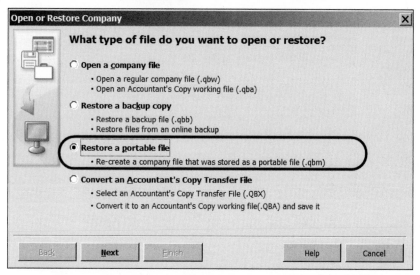

4. If necessary, go to the location of your USB drive and open the
   Your Name QB Backups folder.

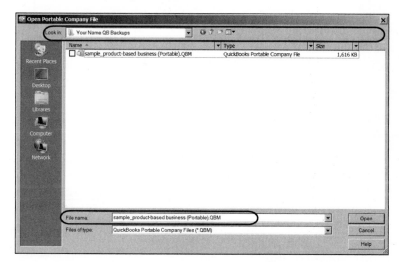

5. Double click on sample_product based business (Portable) to open it.

6. Read the Where do you want to restore the file screen and then click 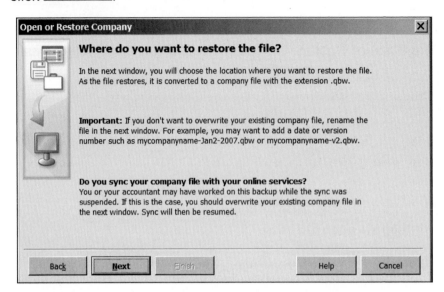.

7. Type Your first and last name in front of File name. Click Save.

8. The following screen appears, Be very patient...opening the portable company file will take several minutes.

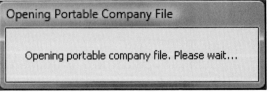

9.   When the QuickBooks Information window appears, click .

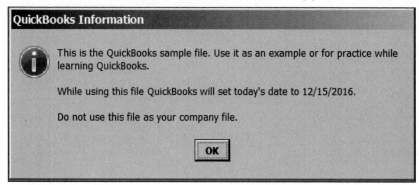

10. When the QuickBooks portable company file has been opened successfully window appears, click 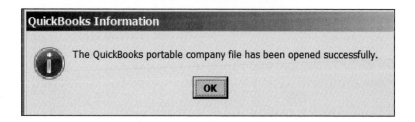.

You are restored to the Sample Rock Castle Construction – QuickBooks 2012 desktop. In order to make sure the Accountant Center window does not open each time, uncheck Show Accountant Center when opening a company file. Then, close the Accountant Center window.

OVERVIEW OF QUICKBOOKS 2012

GRAPHICAL USER INTERFACE (GUI)

The general look of a program is called its graphical user interface. As you know, most programs include the mouse pointer, icons, toolbars, menus, and a navigation bar. QuickBooks' GUI is shown on the next page.

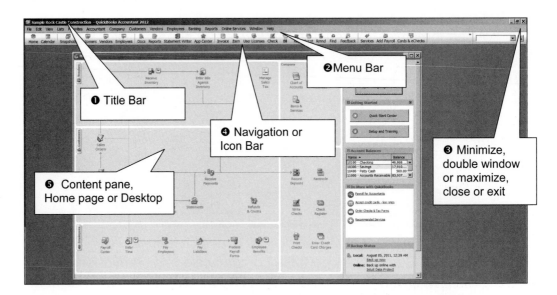

The Sample Rock Castle Construction – QuickBooks 2012 window shows how QB windows are organized. In this textbook, you will use both menu bar selections and Navigation bar selections.

For now, let's study the parts of the window. Some features are common to all software programs using Windows. For example, in the upper right corner is the Minimize ▬ button, Double Window ▣ button, and the Close ✕ button. The title bar, window border, and mouse pointer are also common to Windows programs. Other features are specific to QB: menu bar, icon bar, and navigation bar. Windows programs use menus in the form of horizontal menu bar selections. The contents of these menus differ depending on the application.

❶ **Title Bar:** Contains the company name and the program name, QuickBooks 2012. Sample Rock Castle Construction - QuickBooks Accountant 2012

❷ **Menu Bar:** Contains the menus for File, Edit, View, Lists, Company, Customers, Vendors, Employees, Banking, Reports, Online Services, Window, and Help. You can click with your left-mouse button on the menu bar headings to see its selections.

File   Edit   View   Lists   Favorites   Accountant   Company   Customers   Vendors   Employees   Banking   Reports   Online Services   Window   Help

❸ Minimize ▬, Double Window ▣, or Maximize ▢, and Close or Exit ✕ buttons: Clicking once on Minimize ▬ reduces the window to a button on the **taskbar**. In Windows, the [start] or [⊞] button and taskbar are located at the bottom of your window. Clicking once on Double Window [⧉] returns the window to its previous size. This button appears when you maximize the window. After clicking on the Double Window [⧉] button, the symbol changes to the Maximize [□] button. Click once on the Maximize [□] button to enlarge the window. Click once on the Exit or Close [✕] button to close the window, or exit the program.

❹ *Navigation or Icon Bar*: QuickBooks 2012 offers a graphical alternative to the menu bar. The Navigation Bar contains quick Navigation buttons to Home, Company Snapshots, Customers, Vendors, Employees, Docs, Reports, Statement Writer, App Center, Add Payroll, Cards & eChecks, Services, and Feedback.

❺ *Content Pane, Home Page or Desktop:* Displays information on the company. The following content appears when the Company Home page opens: Vendors, Customers, Employees, Company, Banking and their accompanying workflow processes. The Home page also includes Getting Started, Account Balances, Do More with QuickBooks and Backup Status.

TYPICAL QUICKBOOKS 2012 WINDOWS AND NAVIGATION

The Navigation Bar contains the buttons to quickly access information about customers, vendors, employees, reports, online banking, and help. When one of the Navigation Bar's buttons (Snapshots, Customers, Vendors, Employees, Docs, Reports, Statement Writer, App Center, etc.) is selected, an information rich page appears. For example, click

[Customers], and the Customer Center window is shown. Compare your Customer Center window to the one shown on the next page.

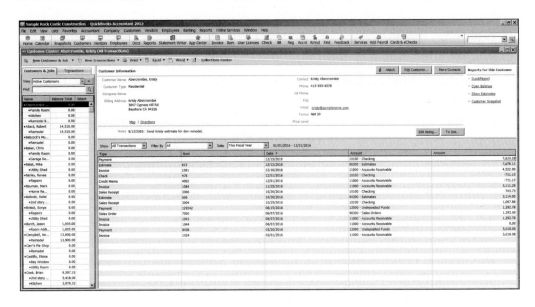

On the left side of the window, explore different views: All Customers, Active Customers, Customers with Open Balances, etc. Click on both the Customer & Job tab and the Transactions tab to see the same customer data presented different ways. Select a customer to view their information and transactions on the right side of the window.

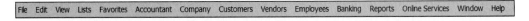

Click with your left-mouse button on the menu bar headings to see the selections. Notice how easily information can be exported to Excel.

MENU BAR

Sample Rock Castle Construction menu bar has 15 selections: File, Edit, View, Lists, Favorites, Accountant, Company, Customers, Vendors, Employees, Banking, Reports, Online Services, Window, and Help.

1. From the menu bar, click File to see the file menu options. The file menu includes selections for New Company, Open or Restore Company, Open Previous Company, Open Second Company, Create Backup, Restore a Previous Local Backup, Create Copy, Close Company, Switch to Multi-user Mode, Utilities, Accountant's Copy, Print Report, Save as PDF (is active when report is selected),

Print Forms, Printer Setup, Send Forms, Shipping, Update Web Services, Toggle to Another Edition, and Exit. If any of the items are grayed out, they are inactive.

An arrow (▶) next to a menu item (for example, Utilities) indicates that there are additional selections. Also, observe that pressing **<Ctrl>+<P>** can be used to Print selected items.

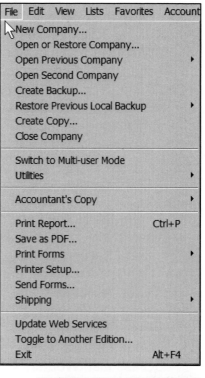

2.   From the Home page's menu bar, click Edit. The edit menu includes selections for Undo Typing (inactive on this illustration), Revert, Cut, Copy, Paste, New Invoice, Delete Invoice, Duplicate Invoice, Memorize Invoice, Void Invoice, Go to Transfer, Transaction History, Mark Invoice as Pending, Notepad, Change Account Color, Use Register, Use Calculator, Find Invoices, Search and Preferences. If grayed out, this means that choice is inactive for the window. Observe that keyboard shortcuts such as **<Ctrl>+ <X>** can be used to Cut. (*Hint:* To see these Edit selections, the Create Invoices window was opened with a customer invoice displayed.)

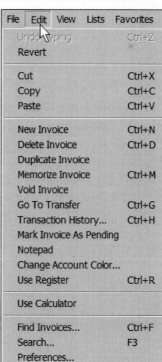

3. From the Home page's menu bar, click View. The View menu allows you to Open Window List, do a Search (Search Box is checked), show the Icon bar (checked), Customize Icon Bar, Add "Home" to Icon Bar, show Favorites Menu (checked), show One Window, or Multiple Windows (selected).

4. From the Home page's menu bar, click Lists. The Lists menu bar has selections for Chart of Accounts, Item List, Fixed Asset Item List, U/M Set List, Price Level List, Billing Rate Level List, Sales Tax Code List, Payroll Item List, Class List, Workers Comp List, Other Names List, Customer & Vendor Profile Lists, Templates, Memorized Transaction List, and Add/Edit Multiple List Entries. An arrow (▶) next to a menu item (for example, Customer & Vendor Profiles Lists) indicates that there are additional selections. Also, observe that pressing **<Ctrl>+<A>** can be used to display the Chart of Accounts.

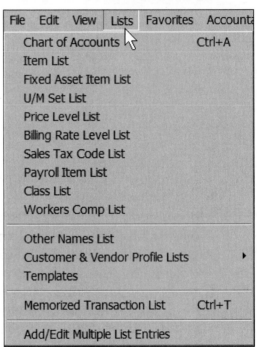

5. From the Home page's menu bar, click Favorites. The Favorites menu allows you to Customize Favorites.

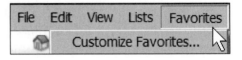

6. From the Menu Bar, select Accountant. The Accountant menu selections include Accountant Center, Chart of Accounts, Fixed Asset Item List, Client Data Review, Make General Journal Entries, Reconcile, Working Trial Balance, Set Closing Date, Condense Data, Remote Access, Manage Fixed Assets, QuickBooks File Manager, ProAdvisor Program, and Online Accountant Resources.

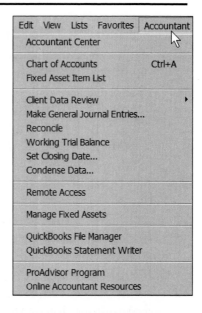

7. From the menu bar, click Company. This selection includes Home Page, Company Snapshot, Calendar, Documents, Lead Center, Company Information, Advanced Service Administration, Set Up Users and Passwords, Customer Credit Card Protection, Set Closing Date, Planning & Budgeting, To Do List, Reminders, Alerts Manager, Chart of Accounts, Make General Journal Entries, Manage Currency, Enter Vehicle Mileage, and Prepare Letters with Envelopes. An arrow (▶) next to a menu item (for example, Set Up Users and Passwords) indicates that there are additional selections.

8. Click on Customers to see its menu. This selection includes Customer Center, Create Estimates, Create Sales Orders, Sales Order Fulfillment Worksheet, Create Invoices, Create Batch Invoices, Enter Sales Receipts, Enter Statement Charges, Create Statements, Assess Finance Charges, Receive Payments, Create Credit Memos/Refunds, Lead Center, Add Credit Card Processing, Add Electronic Check Processing, Link Payment Service to Company File, Enter Time, Item List, and Change Item Prices. An arrow (▶) next to a menu item (for example, Enter Time) indicates that there are additional selections. Also, observe that pressing **\<Ctrl>+\<J>** can be used to display the Customer Center.

Favorites	Accountant	Company	Customers
Customer Center			Ctrl+J
Create Estimates			
Create Sales Orders			
Sales Order Fulfillment Worksheet			
Create Invoices			Ctrl+I
Create Batch Invoices			
Enter Sales Receipts			
Enter Statement Charges			
Create Statements...			
Assess Finance Charges			
Receive Payments			
Create Credit Memos/Refunds			
Lead Center			
Add Credit Card Processing			
Add Electronic Check Processing			
Link Payment Service to Company File			
Enter Time			▶
Item List			
Change Item Prices			

9. Click on Vendors to see its menu. This selection includes Vendor Center, Enter Bills, Pay Bills, Sales Tax, Create Purchase Orders, Receive Items and Enter Bill, Receive Items, Enter Bill for Received Items, Inventory Activities, Print/E-file 1099s, and Item List. An arrow (▶) next to a menu item (for example, Sales Tax) indicates that there are additional selections.

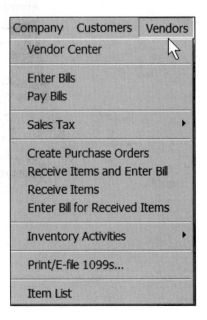

Company	Customers	Vendors
Vendor Center		
Enter Bills		
Pay Bills		
Sales Tax		▶
Create Purchase Orders		
Receive Items and Enter Bill		
Receive Items		
Enter Bill for Received Items		
Inventory Activities		▶
Print/E-file 1099s...		
Item List		

10. Click Employees. This selection includes Employee Center, Payroll Center, Enter Time, Pay Employees, After-the-Fact Payroll, Add or Edit Payroll Schedules, Edit/Void Paychecks, Payroll Taxes and Liabilities, Payroll Tax Forms & W-2s, Intuit 401K, Workers Compensation, Intuit Health Benefits, My Payroll Service, Pay with Direct Deposit, Pay with Pay Card, Payroll Setup, Manage Payroll Items, Get Payroll Updates, and Billing Rate Level List. An arrow (▶) next to a menu item (for example, Enter Time) indicates that there are additional selections.

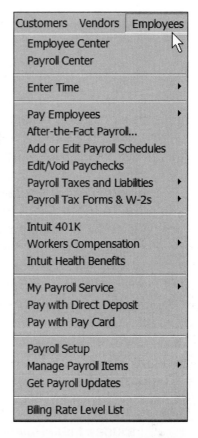

11. Click Banking. This selection includes Write Checks, Order Checks & Envelopes, Enter Credit Card Charges, Use Register, Make Deposits, Transfer Funds, Reconcile, Online Banking, Loan Manager, and Other Names List. An arrow (▶) next to a menu item (for example, Online Banking) indicates that there are additional selections. Also, observe that pressing **<Ctrl>+<W>** can be used to Write Checks and **<Ctrl>+<R>** to Use Register.

12. Click Reports. This selection includes Report Center; Memorized Reports; Company Snapshot; Process Multiple Reports; QuickBooks Statement Writer; Company & Financial; Customers & Receivables; Sales; Jobs, Time & Mileage; Vendors & Payables; Purchases; Inventory; Employees & Payroll; Banking; Accountant & Taxes; Budgets & Forecasts; List; Industry Specific; Contributed Reports; Custom Reports; Quick Report; Transaction History; and Transaction Journal. An arrow (▶) next to a menu item (for example, Company & Financial) indicates that there are additional selections.

13. Click on Online Services. This selection includes Intuit PaymentNetwork, Mobile & Online Access, Manage Services, Get a website, Set Up Intuit Sync Manager, and Manage Apps and Services.

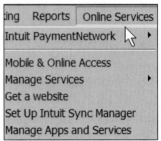

14. Click Window. This selection includes Arrange Icons, Close All, Tile Vertically, Tile Horizontally, Cascade, 1 Home, 2 Create Invoices. (1 and 2 indicate open windows.)

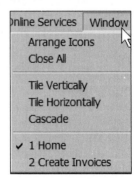

15.   Click Help. This selection includes QuickBooks Help, Ask Intuit, Find Training, Learning Center Tutorials, Support, Find A Local QuickBooks Expert, Send Feedback Online, Recommend QuickBooks, Internet Connection Setup, Year-End Guide, Add QuickBooks Services, App Center:Find More Business Solutions, Update QuickBooks, Manage My License, Manage Data Sync, QuickBooks Privacy Statement, About Automatic Update, and About QuickBooks 2012. An arrow (▶) next to a menu item indicates that there are additional selections. Notice QuickBooks Help can also be accessed from the function key **<F1>**.

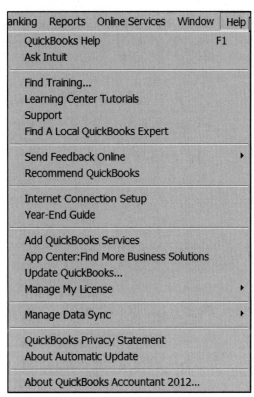

HELP, PREFERENCES, AND PRODUCT INFORMATION

QuickBooks 2012 Help

QuickBooks 2012 includes a lot of user support or help. The instructions that follow demonstrate Help files.

1.   From the QB menu bar, click Help; QuickBooks Help.

2.   The Have a Question? window appears. Notice you can type in a question, then click the Search icon to learn more. Also, notice that a question mark icon appears at the bottom of your screen on the taskbar -

3.   From the Have a Question? window you have choices, you can type a question, or link to various parts of the screen.

4. For example purposes, type **How to get help** in the Search field, then click 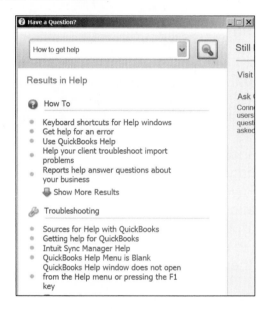.

5. From this window, you can link to various choices. For example, if you choose Use QuickBooks Help, this Help article appears.

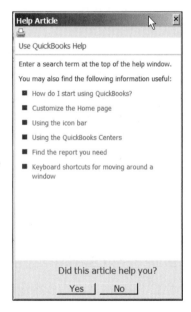

6. Read the information on the Help Article screen. In response to the information provided, you can also select <Yes> or <No>, and provide feedback. When finished, close the Help Article and Have a Question? windows.

Company Preferences

Follow these steps to look at the User and Company Preferences for Sample Rock Castle Construction.

1. From the menu bar, select Edit; Preferences. The Preferences window appears. If necessary, click on the Company Preferences tab. Select a variety of topics on the left side of the screen to view or change preferences. For example, view General preferences. Read the information on the Company Preferences window. Observe where the checkmarks are placed.

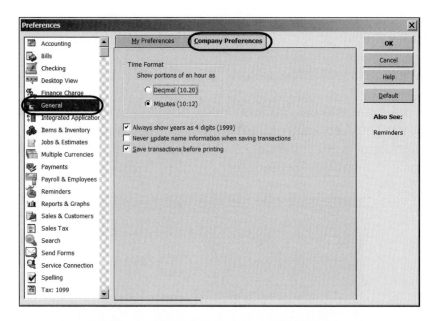

2. Click on My Preferences tab to see user preferences. Select a variety of topics on the left side of the screen to view or change preferences. For example, view General preferences. Read the information on the Company Preferences window. Observe where the checkmarks are placed.

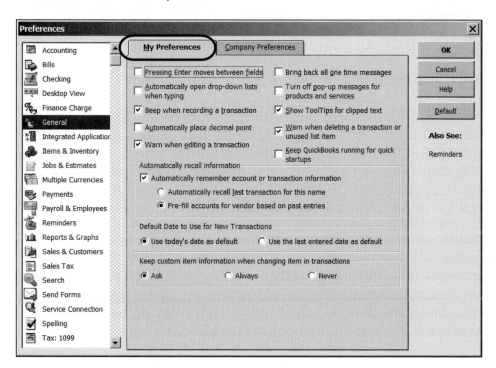

3. Close the window, click ☒ on the Preferences title bar.

Displaying Product Information

1. From the menu bar, click on Help; About QuickBooks Accountant 2012. The About QuickBooks 2012 window appears. (Your License Number, Product Number, and User Licenses will be completed.)

2. After reviewing the window, click the <Esc> key to close.

INTERNAL CONTROL FEATURES

Security Roles and Permissions

Having user roles with defined permissions allows QB to keep sensitive financial data secure and maintain good company internal controls. Good internal controls reduce a business' risk for wrongdoing and fraud by limiting what users can do or view. Users with administrative rights have full access to all aspects of the software including setting up what other users can view or do in QB. Each user can be permitted different authorized access to QB by the administrator. In this text, since you are the administrator, you can set up users and grant them permissions.

The QB Administrator can give a user access to any or all of these areas when a user's password is set up: sales and accounts receivable, purchases and accounts payable, checking and credit cards, inventory, time tracking, payroll, sensitive accounting activities, and sensitive financial reports. (*Hint:* Using QB Help, type **roles** in the search field. Then, link to Access permissions in QuickBooks.)

Add User Roles

To add a role, follow these steps:

1. From Sample Rock Castle Construction menu bar: Company; Set Up Users and Passwords, Set Up Users.

2. The User List box appears. Click on Add User…You will be adding the Cashier role. A cashier enters customer purchases and collects cash payments or credit card payments from customers. For example, a grocery store cashier, store sales clerk, or restaurant wait staff.

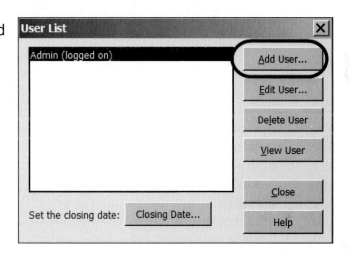

3. In Set up user password and access window, type User Name: **Cashier**. Click Next > . When the No Password Entered window appears, click No . If you type a password, the authors suggest cashier. (*Hint:* If you type a password, it will need to be entered when the backup file is restored.)

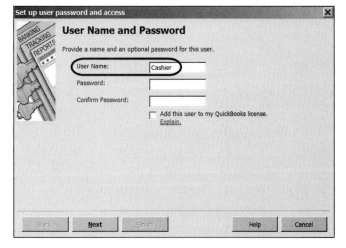

4. In Access for user: Cashier window, pick "Selected areas of QuickBooks" to separate cashier from duties not specific to their job. Click 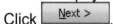.

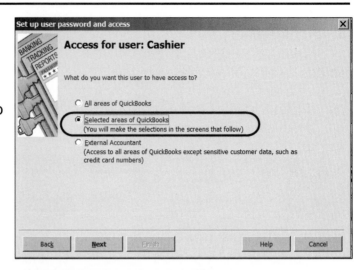

5. In Sales and Accounts Receivable window, since cashiers process customer payments and give customers receipts, the cashier must have selective access to create and print

transactions only. Click 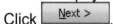.

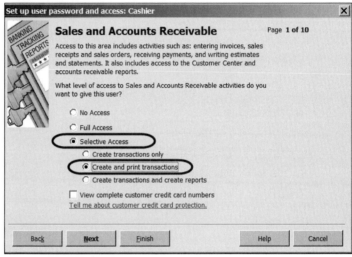

6. In Purchases and Accounts Payable window, select No Access. Good internal control separates the duties of cash collection from cash payments. Click 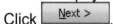.

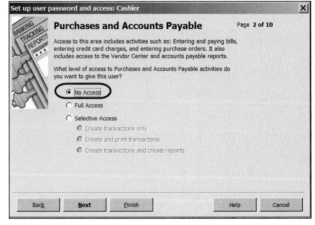

7. In Checking and Credit Cards window, select No Access. Good internal control assigns different employees the task of making bank deposits versus processing customer payments. Click [Next >].

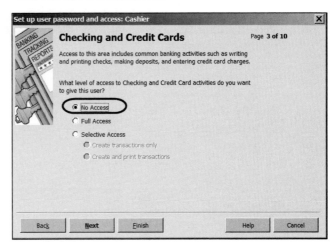

8. In Inventory, select No Access. Continue selecting No Access for Time Tracking, Payroll and Employees, Sensitive Accounting Activities, and Sensitive Financial Reporting. Click [Next >] between each window.

9. In Changing or Deleting Transactions window, select No for both questions since good internal control generally requires supervisor authorization of any changes. Click [Next >].

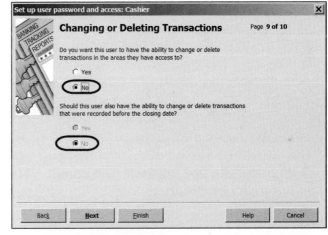

10. Review access for user: Cashier, make any changes by clicking <Back> if necessary. Observe that you are on Page 10 of 10. Click [**Finish**].

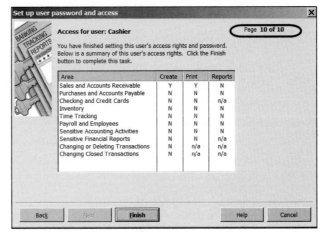

11. When the Warning window appears, read the information, then click 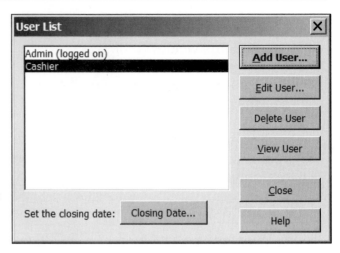 OK . Notice the User List now contains two user roles, Admin and Cashier. Click Close to return to the QuickBooks desktop.

EXTERNAL ACCOUNTANT REVIEWS

When a company wants their external accountant to review their accounting records, the accountant generally must physically visit the business. With QB Accountant features, a physical visit is no longer necessary and both the company and the accountant can continue to work simultaneously with the data. Company data can be shared with the accountant various ways. It can be shared using a CD or USB flash drive, or sent via e-mail as an attachment, or uploaded to a shared secure website. In this text, your Accountant is your professor. Periodically throughout the text, you will be sending your company files via e-mail to your professor. In other words, you will be submitting your work for grading purposes. For example, in Exercise 2-1 you will send an e-mail attachment to your professor.

AUDIT TRAIL

Software programs generally have an audit trail feature to keep track of users accessing the software, when they are using it, and what they are doing in the software. An audit trail is another internal control feature of QuickBooks which documents all business activities to keep company data safe. Periodically in this text, you will be printing your audit trail and submitting it to your professor to document your work. To create and view the audit trail of the sample product company, follow these steps.

1. From Sample Rock Castle Construction menu bar: Reports; Accountant & Taxes, Audit Trail.

2. The Audit Trail is displayed. Review the type of information an audit trail provides and how the report can be customized. Observe that the Date Entered/Last Modified field shows Today; and that the From and To fields show 12/15/2016. That's the date assigned to the sample company. Close the Audit Trail report.

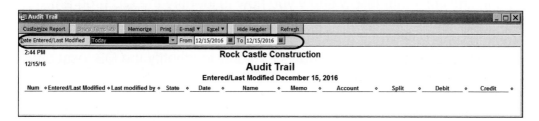

CHAPTER 2 DATA BACK UP

At the end of each chapter, the authors recommend that you backup. Backing up insures that you have data to restore if you make a mistake or are transporting your work between computer labs. For example, let's say you would like to start Sample Rock Castle Construction from the beginning. The backup made early this chapter, sample_product-based business (Portable).QBM, contains fresh, starting data. If you back up your work now and restore the backup file made below (Your Name Chapter 2 End (Portable).QBM, you can start the sample company from the end of this chapter.

Follow the steps in this chapter to back up your work now. (*HINT:* From the menu bar, select File; Create Copy. When the Save Copy or Backup window appears, select Portable company file for the type of file you want to save.)

Name **Your Name Chapter 2 End (Portable)** i.e., First and Last Name Chapter 2 End, in the File name field and save it on your USB drive.

Click on [X] to exit Sample Rock Castle Construction and return to the windows desktop, or continue.

USING WINDOWS EXPLORER

The instructions that follow show you how to identify the QB program path, directories, and subdirectories on the hard drive of your computer. You also see the size of the QB and its associated files and folders. Follow these steps to use Windows Explorer to identify the QB location on your computer system.

1. If necessary, minimize QuickBooks 2012. Your Windows desktop should be displayed.

2. If your desktop has a Windows Explorer icon [ ], click on it. *Or,* right click [Start], left-click Open Windows Explorer; or [ ]; Explore All Users. Select drive C, then double-click on the Program Files (x86) folder to open it. (If you are using Vista or XP, open the Program Files folder. These instructions were done with Windows 7.) The address field shows Computer, Local Disk (C), Program Files (x86). Now locate double-click on the Intuit folder so that the Address field shows Computer, Local Disk (C), Program Files (x86), Intuit. This is the location (program path) of QuickBooks 2012 on your computer.

3. Notice that the right pane on your computer shows the folders for QuickBooks 2012.

4. Right-click on the QuickBooks 2012 folder. A drop-down list appears. Left-click on Properties. The QuickBooks 2012 Properties window appears. Compare your QuickBooks 2012 Properties window to the one shown on the next page. Your files sizes may differ. The date shown in the Created field will also differ.

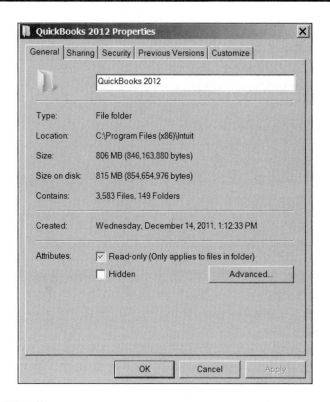

5. Click [OK] to close the QuickBooks 2012 Properties window.
    Close Windows Explorer.

SUMMARY AND REVIEW

OBJECTIVES:

1. Start QuickBooks 2012 (QB).
2. Open the sample product-based business,
3. Backup and restore the sample business.
4. Overview of QuickBooks 2012.
5. QuickBooks Help, Preferences, and Product Information.
6. QuickBooks Internal Control features.
7. Using Windows Explorer.

RESOURCEFUL QUICKBOOKS

Read Me: QUICKBOOKS LEARNING CENTER

From the QuickBooks desktop, Select
Help; Learning Center Tutorials.

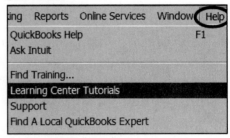

Watch the QuickBooks
Learning Center video
tutorials about
Overview & Setup then
answer the following
questions. *(You will
need speakers or
headphones to hear the
tutorial.)*

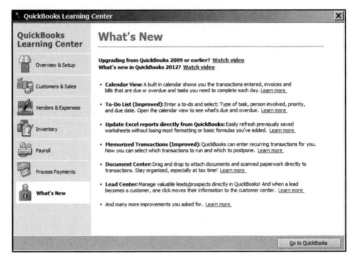

1. What topics did
    Getting around in
    QuickBooks video
    cover in detail?

2. In Overview of QuickBooks accounts video, what financial statement
    does QuickBooks call by a different name?

3. In Overview of QuickBooks accounts video, what are the 5 kinds of
    accounts? What financial reports do they appear in?

Multiple Choice Questions: The Online Learning Center includes the multiple-choice questions at www.mhhe.com/QBessentials2012, select Student Edition, Chapter 2, Multiple Choice.

_____1. How do you check your software registration status?

     a. Select File; Restore previous backup.
     b. Select Edit; Preferences.
     c. Software is automatically registered.
     d. With company open, press <F2>.

_____2. What happens to the QuickBooks Student Trial Edition once the trial period expires?

     a. Becomes QuickBooks Online Edition.
     b. Becomes QuickBooks Basic Edition.
     c. Becomes QuickBooks Premier Edition.
     d. Becomes inoperable.

_____3. When using the sample companies today's date is set to:

     a. 12/15/2013.
     b. 12/15/2014.
     c. 12/15/2015.
     d. 12/15/2016.

_____4. QuickBooks Student Trial Edition can be backed up to:

     a. Hard drive.
     b. Network drive.
     c. External media.
     d. All of the above.

_____5. Back up files may be saved as:

     a. Back up copy.
     b. Portable company file.
     c. Accountant copy.
     d. All of the above.

_____6. Which of the following appears on the Menu Bar:

    a. Help.
    b. Find.
    c. Search.
    d. Feedback.

_____7. All of the following Centers appear on the Navigation Bar except:

    a. Customer Center.
    b. Employee Center.
    c. Help Center.
    d. Vendor Center.

_____8. The File menu contains all the following except:

    a. Exit.
    b. Preferences.
    c. Utilities.
    d. All of the above.

_____9. The Edit menu contains all the following except:

    a. Use Register.
    b. Preferences.
    c. Use Calculator.
    d. List.

_____10. The Reports menu contains all the following except:

    a. Loans.
    b. Purchases.
    c. Inventory.
    d. Budgets.

Short-answer questions: To answer these questions, go online to
www.mhhe.com/QBessentials2012, link to Student Edition, Chapter 2,
QA Templates. The analysis question on the next page is also included.

1. What are the names of the two sample businesses?

2. What is the purpose of Backup and Restore?

3. List Navigation Bar buttons.

4. How can a user access QuickBooks Help?

5. Preferences can be customized two ways, list them.

6. List steps to display QuickBooks product information.

7. What rights and permissions does a QuickBooks Administrator
    have?

8. When a user is set up, list some of the access rights that can be
    granted.

9. Why is an audit trail important for good internal control?

10. What Windows program is used to view QuickBooks 2012
    properties?

Exercise 2-1: Follow the instructions below to complete Exercise 2-1:

1.   Start QB. (*Hint:* If Rock Castle
     Construction is shown on your title
     bar, select File; Close
     Company/Logoff). Open the sample
     service-based business. The title bar
     shows Sample Larry's Landscaping
     & Garden Supply - QuickBooks
     2012.

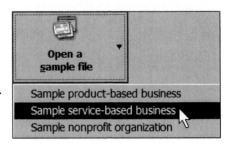

2.   Backup the sample service-based business to the USB drive folder
     named Your Name QB Backups. The suggested backup file name
     is **Your Name sample_service-based business**. Use your first
     and last name. (*Hint*: On the Save Copy or Backup window, select
     Portable company file.)

3.   Click on [X] to exit the sample service-based business and
     return to the windows desktop.

Exercise 2-2: Follow the instructions below to complete Exercise 2-2.

1.   Start your e-mail program.

2.   Create an e-mail message to your professor. Type **Your Name
     Chapter 2 End** for the Subject. (Use your first and last name.)

3.   Attach the file you backed on page 55 called **Your Name Chapter 2
     End (Portable)**. Recall it is located on your USB drive. (*Hint:* If you
     created a password, remember to send to instructor. If you did <u>not</u>
     create a password, when the file is restored a QuickBooks Login
     window appears. Select [OK] to restore the file.)

4.   CC yourself on the message to be sure the message sends.

5.   Send the message to your professor. You should receive a copy of
     it as well.

ANALYSIS QUESTION: Why is it important to set up user roles and
permissions?

Chapter 3
New Company Setup for a Merchandising Business

OBJECTIVES: In Chapter 3, you learn to:

1. Open company called Your Name Retailers Inc.
2. Set preferences.
3. Edit the chart of accounts.
4. Enter beginning balances.
5. Record check register entries.
6. Edit to correct an error.
7. Complete account reconciliation.
8. Display the trial balance.
9. Display the financial statements.
10. Make backup of work.[1]

Additional textbook related resources are on the textbook website at www.mhhe.com/QBessentials2012. The website includes chapter resources, including troubleshooting tips, online quizzes, QA templates, etc.

In this text you are the sole stockholder and manager of a merchandising corporation that sells inventory. Merchandising businesses are retail stores that resell goods and services.

In this chapter, you open your merchandising business called Your Name Retailers Inc. that you set up in Chapter 1. Then, you complete the accounting tasks for the month of October using your checkbook register and bank statement as source documents.

In accounting, you learn that source documents are used to show written evidence of a business transaction. In this chapter the source documents used are your checkbook register and bank statement.

---

[1]The chart in the Preface, page xii, shows the file name and size of each backup file. Refer to this chart for backing up data. Remember, you can back up to a hard drive location or external media.

The McGraw-Hill Companies, Inc., *Computer Accounting Essentials with QuickBooks 2012*

GETTING STARTED

1. Start QuickBooks 2012 from desktop by double clicking on icon.

2. You should see Your Name Retailers Inc. on the title bar.

    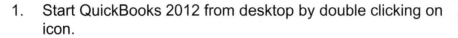

    a. If not, Select File; Close Company. In No Company Open pane, click on Open or restore an existing company button.

    b. In Open or Restore window, select Restore a backup copy. Click Next.

    c. Select Local backup. Click Next.

    d. Browse your external media and select the Your Name Retailers Inc. backup that you made in Chapter 1, pages 18-20. (Your date will differ.)

    e. Click Open. In the Where do you want to restore the file? window, click Next.

    f. Rename Your Name Retailers Inc. to **Your Name Retailers Inc. Chapter 3** in the Save Company File window.

    g. Click Save. When the screen prompts "Your data has been restored successfully," click OK. The title bar shows

h. If a QuickBooks Learning Center window appears, click
Go to QuickBooks .

3. On your QuickBooks desktop, click on
⊞ **Account Balances** to view the cash
balance in Home State Bank of $0.00.

⊟ Account Balances	
Name ▲	Balance
Home State Bank	0.00

COMPANY PREFERENCES

Follow these steps to set the company preferences for Your Name
Retailers Inc.

1. From the menu bar,
select Edit; Preferences.
Click on Company
Preferences tab and
select Accounting.

2. Check the box next to
Use account numbers.
Uncheck the boxes next
to Date Warnings.
Compare your screen
with the one shown here.

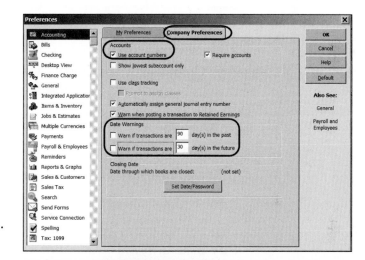

3. Click **OK** .

4. From the menu bar,
select Edit; Preferences.
Click on My Preferences
tab; Desktop View.
Select a Color Scheme
of your choice. Click
OK .

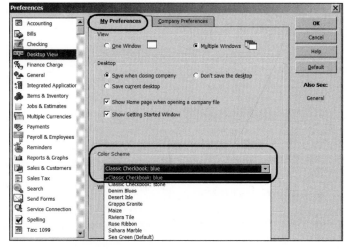

5. From the menu bar,
select Edit; Preferences.
Click on My Preferences
tab, Checking. Put a check mark next to "Open the Write Checks

form with...account," the "Open the Pay Bills form with...account," and "Open the Make Deposits form with...account." Compare your screen to the one shown here.

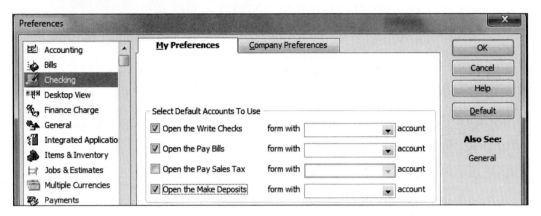

a. For "Open the Write Checks form with....account," use the pulldown menu to select the **Home State Bank** account.

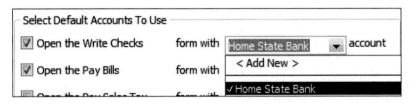

b. Use the pulldown menu to pick **Home State Bank** for "Open the Pay Bills form with...account" and "Open the Make Deposits form with...account. Then, click **OK** .

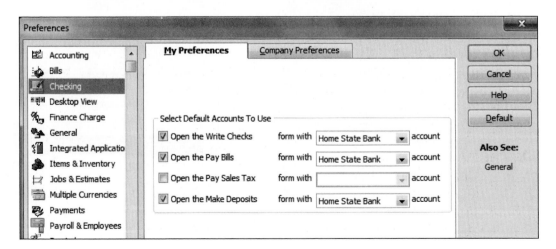

6. From the Menu Bar, select Edit; Preferences. Click on My Preferences tab and select Send Forms. Uncheck box next to "Auto-check the "To be e-mailed" checkbox if customer's Preferred Send Method is e-mail." If necessary, select Web Mail in the Send e-mail using area. Click OK .

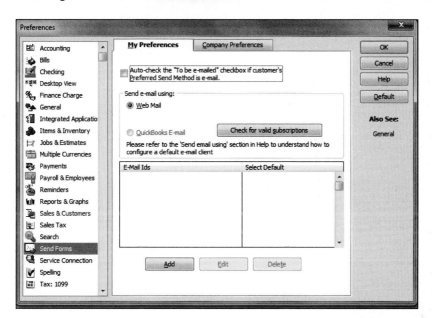

When the Warning window appears, read it, then click OK . Click to see the Home page.

CHART OF ACCOUNTS

Examine the Home page to learn there are many ways to access a company's chart of accounts. In accounting you learn that the chart of accounts is a list of all accounts in the company's general ledger. Notice you can click on the desktop icon; use the Smart Key <Ctrl><A>; or from the Menu Bar select either Lists; Chart of Accounts, or Company; Chart of Accounts.

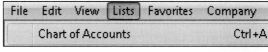

1. From Desktop, click on the Chart of Accounts icon. If a popup box appears about new features, click OK .

2.   The Chart of Accounts appears. Resize so you can view all accounts. Notice all have 0.00 balance totals.

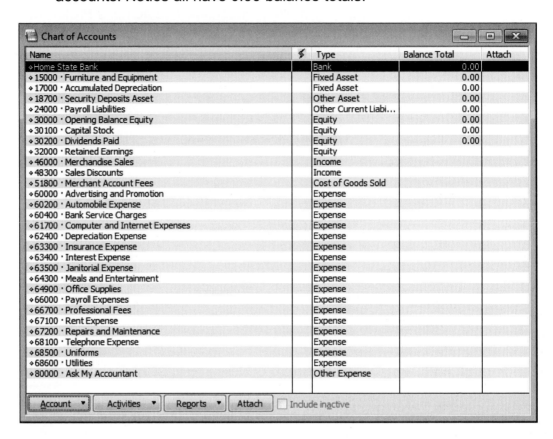

Follow these steps to add, edit, and change accounts.

Delete Accounts

Follow these steps to delete accounts.

1.   Highlight Account No. 48300, Sales Discounts. From Menu Bar select Edit; Delete Account. Notice you can also use the Smart Key <Ctrl> <D> to delete an account.

2.   When the window prompts "Are you sure that you want to delete this account?," click [OK] Account No. 48300, Sales Discounts, is removed.

3. Your Name Retailers Inc. chart of accounts is extensive. For now, delete the accounts shown on the table below.

No.	Name
18700	Security Deposits Asset
63500	Janitorial Expense
64300	Meals and Entertainment
66700	Professional Fees
68500	Uniforms
80000	Ask My Accountant

Make Accounts Inactive

Follow these steps to make Account No. 24000, Payroll Liabilities, inactive.

1. Highlight Account No. 24000, Payroll Liabilities and right-click. From the menu, left-click Make Account Inactive.

2. Repeat step 1 to make Account 66000, Payroll Expenses inactive.

3. Check "Include Inactive" box at bottom of the Chart of Accounts to reveal all inactive accounts. Notice inactive accounts have an X beside them.

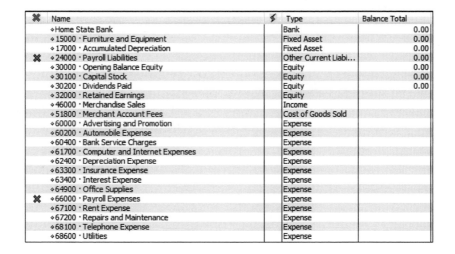

Change/Edit Accounts

Follow these steps to change or edit an account.

1. Right-click on Account No. 30000, Opening Balance Equity.

2. Left-click Edit Account.

3. Change the Account name field to **Common Stock**. Change Description field to **Common Stock par value.**

4. For Tax-Line Mapping select: B/S-Liabs/Eq.: Capital Stock-Common Stock.

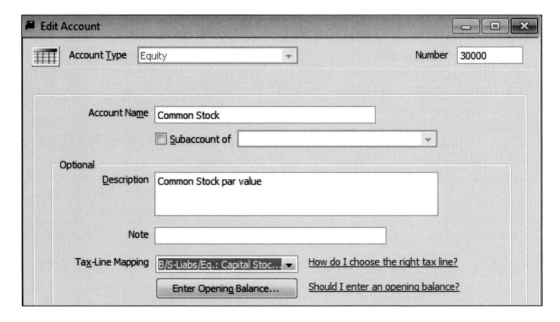

5. Click Save & Close. Observe that Account No. 30000 name is Common Stock.

6. Change the following accounts.

No.	New Name	Change
30100	Paid in Capital	Description: Paid in Capital Tax-Line Mapping: B/S-Liabs/Eq.: Paid in or capital surplus.
30200	Dividends	
46000	Sales	
51800	Freight In	Description: FOB shipping
60000	Advertising and Promotion Exp.	
60400	Bank Service Charges Expense	
64900	Supplies Expense	Description: Supplies expense
67200	Repairs and Maintenance Expense	
68600	Utilities	
10000	Home State Bank-Cash (*Hint:* In the Number field, type **10000**)	Description: Cash in bank Tax Line Mapping: B/S-Assets: Cash
17000	Accumulated Depreciation-F&E	Tax Line Mapping: B/S-Assets: Accumulated Depreciation

Add Accounts

1. Display the Chart of Accounts. From your Menu Bar select Edit; New Account. Notice you can also use the Smart Key <Ctrl> <N> to add a new account.

2. To add Account No. 14000, Computer Equipment, select Fixed Asset (major purchases). Click Con**ti**nue.

3. In Number field, type **14000**, in Account Name field type **Computer Equipment.** For Description, type **Computer equipment.**

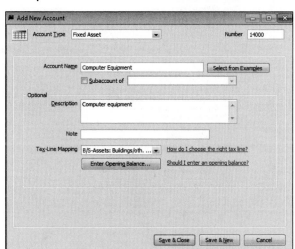

4. When satisfied, click Save & New.

---

5. Add the following accounts.

No.	Name	Account Type	Tax-Line Mapping
13000	Supplies	Other current asset	B/S-Assets: Other current assets
16000	Accumulated Depreciation-CEqmt.	Fixed asset	B/S-Assets: Accumulated Depreciation
18000	Prepaid Insurance	Other current asset	B/S-Assets: Other current assets
22000	Accounts Payable	Accounts Payable	B/S-Liabs/Eq.: Accounts payable
26000	Your Name Notes Payable	Long Term Liability	B/S-Liabs/Eq.: Loans from Stockholders
50000	Cost of Goods Sold	Cost of goods sold	COGS-Schedule A: Purchases

6. When done adding accounts, click **Save & Close**.

7. View your chart of accounts list.

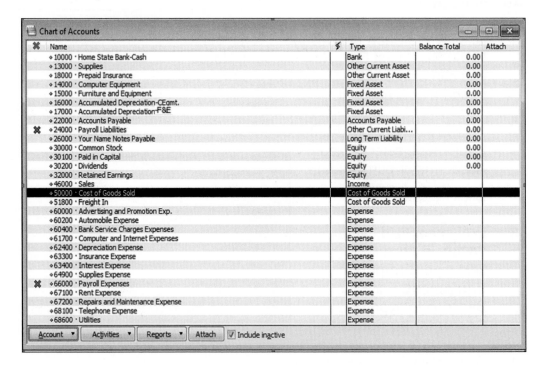

BEGINNING BALANCES

The *Balance Sheet* will establish your beginning balances as of October 1, 20XX (current year). In accounting you learn that a Balance Sheet lists the types and amounts of assets, liabilities, and equity as of a specific date. A balance sheet is also called a *statement of financial position*. Since QuickBooks asks you to enter the account balances on the day prior to your start date, the September 30 balance sheet is shown here.

Your Name Retailers Inc. Balance Sheet, September 30, 20XX (current year)		
ASSETS		
Current Assets:		
10000 - Home State Bank-Cash	$50,000.00	
Other Current Assets:		
13000 - Supplies	2,500.00	
18000 -Prepaid Insurance	2,500.00	
Total Current Assets		$55,000.00
Fixed Assets:		
14000 - Computer Equipment	1,000.00	
15000 - Furniture and Equipment	4,000.00	
Total Fixed Assets		5,000.00
Total Assets		$60,000.00
LIABILITIES AND STOCKHOLDERS' EQUITIES		
Long-Term Liabilities:		
26000 – Your Name Notes Payable	20,000.00	
Total Long-Term Liabilities		$20,000.00
Stockholders' Equities:		
30000 - Common Stock		40,000.00
Total Liabilities & Equities		$60,000.00

Follow the steps shown to enter opening balances for Your Name Retailers Inc. on September 30, 20XX, the day before your QuickBooks start date. If your chart of accounts is not showing on your desktop, click on the Chart of Accounts icon. Notice all accounts have 0.00 balance totals.

1. Right-click on Account No. 13000 Supplies.

2. Select Edit Account.

3. Click on Enter Opening Balance...

4. In Opening Balance field type **2,500.00** as of **09/30/20XX**. **(Use your current year)**. Click OK.

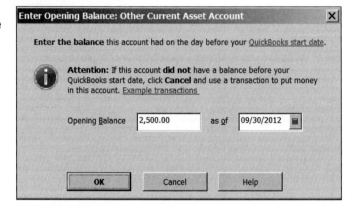

5. When returned to the Edit Account screen, select Save & Close.

6. Edit the following accounts to add their beginning balances:

No.	Name	Opening Balance as of 09/30/20XX
10000	Home State Bank-Cash	50,000.00
14000	Computer Equipment	1,000.00
15000	Furniture and Equipment	4,000.00
18000	Prepaid Insurance	2,500.00
26000	Your Name Notes Payable	20,000.00

7. Compare your chart of accounts to the one shown. Edit yours until it agrees.

✖	Name	⚡	Type	Balance Total
	◆ 10000 · Home State Bank-Cash		Bank	50,000.00
	◆ 13000 · Supplies		Other Current Asset	2,500.00
	◆ 18000 · Prepaid Insurance		Other Current Asset	2,500.00
	◆ 14000 · Computer Equipment		Fixed Asset	1,000.00
	◆ 15000 · Furniture and Equipment		Fixed Asset	4,000.00
	◆ 16000 · Accumulated Depreciation-CEqmt.		Fixed Asset	0.00
	◆ 17000 · Accumulated Depreciation-F&E		Fixed Asset	0.00
	◆ 22000 · Accounts Payable		Accounts Payable	0.00
✖	◆ 24000 · Payroll Liabilities		Other Current Liabi…	0.00
	◆ 26000 · Your Name Notes Payable		Long Term Liability	20,000.00
	◆ 30000 · Common Stock		Equity	40,000.00
	◆ 30100 · Paid in Capital		Equity	0.00
	◆ 30200 · Dividends		Equity	0.00
	◆ 32000 · Retained Earnings		Equity	
	◆ 46000 · Sales		Income	
	◆ 50000 · Cost of Goods Sold		Cost of Goods Sold	
	◆ 51800 · Freight In		Cost of Goods Sold	
	◆ 60000 · Advertising and Promotion Exp.		Expense	
	◆ 60200 · Automobile Expense		Expense	
	◆ 60400 · Bank Service Charges Expenses		Expense	
	◆ 61700 · Computer and Internet Expenses		Expense	
	◆ 62400 · Depreciation Expense		Expense	
	◆ 63300 · Insurance Expense		Expense	
	◆ 63400 · Interest Expense		Expense	
	◆ 64900 · Supplies Expense		Expense	
✖	◆ 66000 · Payroll Expenses		Expense	
	◆ 67100 · Rent Expense		Expense	
	◆ 67200 · Repairs and Maintenance Expense		Expense	
	◆ 68100 · Telephone Expense		Expense	
	◆ 68600 · Utilities		Expense	

October 1 Balance Sheet

To make sure that you have entered the October 1 balances correctly, display a balance sheet and compare it to the balance sheet on the previous page. Follow these steps to do that.

1. From the Navigation Bar, click on the Report Center button **Reports** . Wait while the Report Center opens. (If a New! Contributed reports! window appears, click Close.)

2. On the left pane, select "Company & Financial" then scroll down until you locate Balance Sheet & Net Worth, click on Balance Sheet Standard.

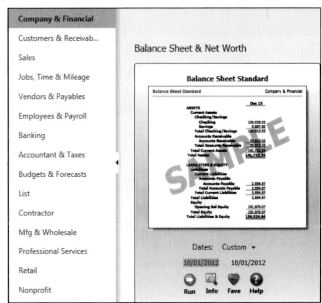

3. For Dates, use pulldown to select "Custom" and Type **10/01/20XX (use current year)** in the Date field or use the calendar to pick the

   date. Click on . The 10/01/20XX balance sheet appears. Compare the account balances to the one shown here (your year may differ).

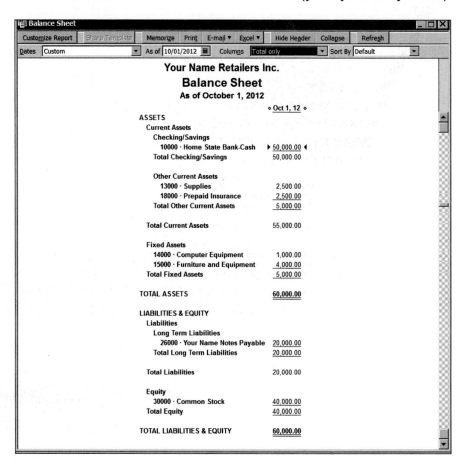

4. From Menu bar, select File; then either Print Report or Save as PDF. If you Save as PDF, browse to your USB drive and name file: **Your Name October 1 BS.pdf.**

5. From the menu bar, select Window, Close All. Click the Home button to return to the Home page.

BACKUP BEGINNING COMPANY DATA

Follow these steps to backup Your Name Retailers Inc. October 1 data.

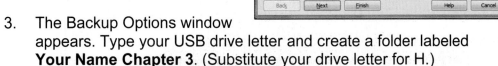

1. From Menu bar, select File; Create Backup.

2. Select "Local backup" and click **Next**.

3. The Backup Options window appears. Type your USB drive letter and create a folder labeled **Your Name Chapter 3**. (Substitute your drive letter for H.)

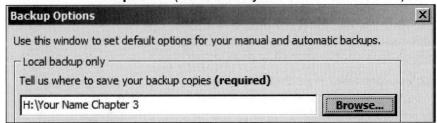

4. Click **OK**. When the screen prompts "The directory you have selected doesn't exist," select **Yes**.

5. Select "Save it now" to question, "When do you want to save your backup copy?" Click **Next**.

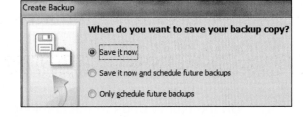

6. The Save Backup Copy window appears. In the File name field, type **Your Name Chapter 3 October 1**. Click **Save**.

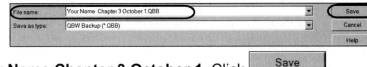

7. When the window prompts, QuickBooks has saved a backup of the company file...., click **OK**. You are returned to the Home page.

ACCOUNT REGISTER

An account register for cash transactions is a listing of all deposits and checks. It is similar to your checkbook register. Your Name Retailers Inc. checkbook is shown here. Your Name Retailers Inc. writes checks and deposits manually in their checkbook and then records them in QuickBooks 2012.

Check Number	Date	Description of Transaction	Payment	Deposit	Balance
					50,000.00
	10/2	Deposit (Acct. No. 30000, Common Stock)		1,500.00	51,500.00
4002	10/4	The Business Store (Acct.14000, Computer Equipment) for computer storage	1,000.00		50,500.00
4003	10/25	Office Supply Store (Acct. No. 13000, Supplies)	200.00		50,300.00

In accounting, you learn that source documents are used to show written evidence of a business transaction. Examples of source documents are sales invoices, purchase invoices, and in this case, the checkbook register for your Home State Bank account.

Make Deposits

Follow these steps to use your checkbook register to record your October entries relating to cash.

1. On the Home page in the Banking section, notice there are task icons to record deposits, write checks, print checks, reconcile bank statement, and view check register.

2. Since the first transaction in your register was a deposit, click on the Record Deposits icon.

3. The Make Deposits window appears. For Deposit To select **10000 Home State Bank-Cash**. For Date enter **10/02/20XX** (your current year). For From Account select **30000 Common Stock**. For Pmt Meth. select **Cash**. For Amount type **1500.00.**

4. For Received From select **<Add New>** . The Select Name Type window appears.

5. In Select Name Type window pick **Other** and then click OK.

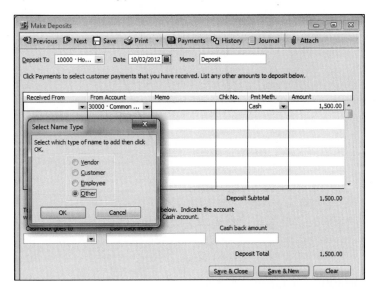

6. The New Name window appears. Type **Your Name, address,** and **phone number.** Click 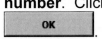.

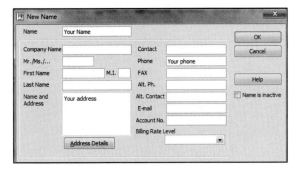

7. The Received From field now shows Your Name. Compare your Make Deposits screen with the one shown on the next page.

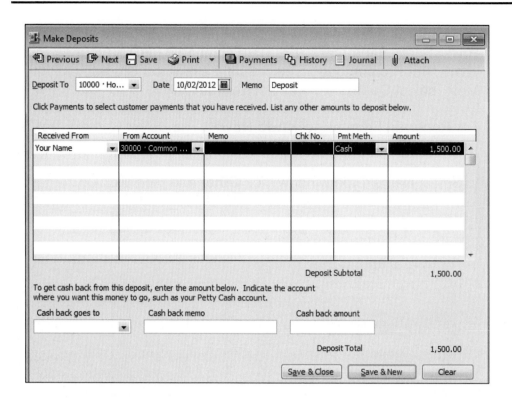

8. Click Save & Close. You are returned to the Home page.

9. Click on the icon for Check Register.

10. Compare your Check Register to the one shown. Notice both the opening cash balance and the 10/2 deposit are shown. The updated cash balance in account 10000 is $51,500.00.

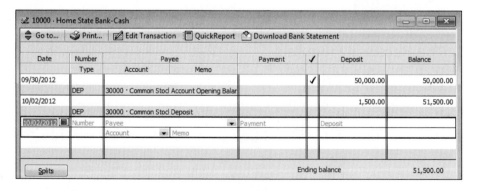

11. To close the Check Register, click ▣.

Write Checks for Assets

Follow these steps to record a purchase of computer storage.

1. From the Home page, click on the icon, Write Checks.

2. The Write Checks window appears. In the Bank Account field, select Account No. 10000, Home State Bank-Cash. Observe that the Ending Balance field shows $51,500. This is the same balance as on the check register shown on the previous page.

3. Click on the To be printed box to uncheck it.

4. Type **4002** in the No. field.

5. Type **10/4/20XX (use your current year)** in the Date field.

6. Type **1000** in the Amount field.

7. In the Pay to the Order of field, select **<Add New>** . The Select Name Type window appears, pick Vendor and click

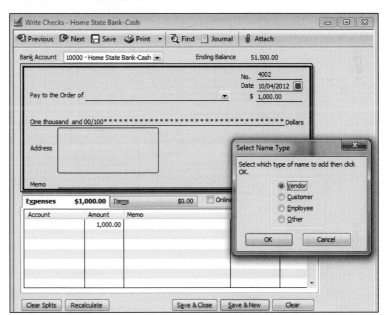

OK .

8. The New Vendor window appears. Type **The Business Store** for Vendor Name, **0.00** for the Opening Balance as of **10/04/20XX** and then click OK .

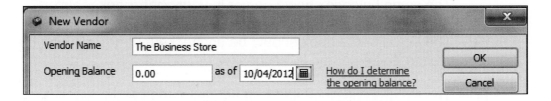

9.   In the Items and expenses table, Expenses should be selected. In the Account field, select Account No. 14000, Computer Equipment. In Memo field type **Computer Storage.**

10. Compare your Check window to the one shown here.

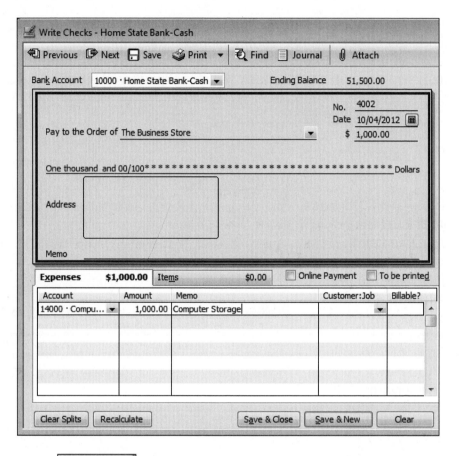

11. Click [Save & New] to begin to record the next check.

12. The Write Checks window appears. In the Bank Account field Account No. 10000, Home State Bank-Cash should appear. If not, select it. Observe that the Ending Balance field shows $50,500.00. The same balance shown earlier in your checkbook register.

13. The To be printed box should be unchecked. (If not, click on the box next to To be printed to uncheck it.)

14. The No. field displays 4003. If not, type **4003** in the No. field.

15.   Type **10/25/20XX (use your current year)** in the Date field.

16.   Type **300** in the Amount field.

17.   In the Pay to field, type **The Office Supply Store**. When the Name Not Found window appears asking to add the payee to the Name list, click [Quick Add]. Add The Office Supply Store as a vendor and click [OK]. You are returned to the Write Checks window.

18.   In Memo field type **Store Supplies.**

19.   In the Items and expenses table, Expenses should be selected. In the Account field, select Account No. 13000, Supplies. The Amount field should show 300.00.

20.   Compare your Check window to the one shown here. Click [Save & Close].

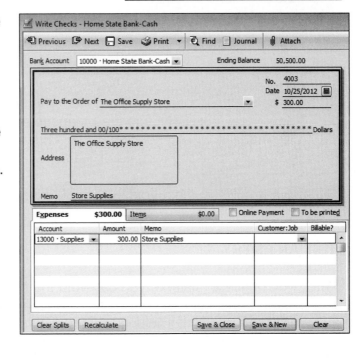

Home State Bank Check Register

Periodically view the check register to confirm the account balance equals what is shown on the checkbook register and that there are no errors.

To view the Check Register, follow these steps.

1.   From the Banking section of the Home page, click on Check Register icon.

---

2. The 10000 Home State Bank-Cash window appears.

Date	Number	Payee		Payment	✓	Deposit	Balance
	Type	Account	Memo				
10/02/2012						1,500.00	51,500.00
	DEP	30000 · Common Stc Deposit					
10/04/2012	4002	The Business Store		1,000.00			50,500.00
	CHK	14000 · Computer Ec					
10/25/2012	4003	The Office Supply Store		300.00			50,200.00
	CHK	13000 · Supplies	Store Supplies				
10/25/2012	Number	Payee		Payment		Deposit	
		Account	Memo				

Ending balance: 50,200.00

Splits

☐ 1-Line

Sort by Date, Type, Number/...

3. Compare the above check register to your checkbook register shown previously. Notice the balances are not the same. An error was made in writing check # 4003. The check was written incorrectly for $300 instead of $200.

4. To correct, you must void the check in your checkbook and edit the entry.

EDIT AN ENTRY

When you notice a mistake, you can void the check in your checkbook and edit the transaction in your Check Register. Since QuickBooks 2012 includes an audit trail, it tracks every transaction and shows when and how an entry was changed. You can view this audit trail using Menu Bar Reports; Accountant & Taxes, Audit Trail. When you void a check and edit a transaction, the audit trail shows the original entry (Prior) and the edited entry (Latest).

Follow these steps to correct the error.

1. You should be viewing the Check Register. If not, from the Banking section of the Home page, click on Check Register icon.

2. Move the mouse to the 10/25 transaction. Click on 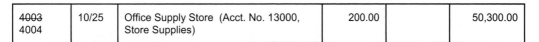. This takes you to the original 10/25 entry. To edit the entry, type the correct check No. **4004** and amount **200.00** over the incorrect entries (*HINT:* Press <Tab> to move between fields.)

4003 4004	10/25	Office Supply Store (Acct. No. 13000, Store Supplies)	200.00		50,300.00

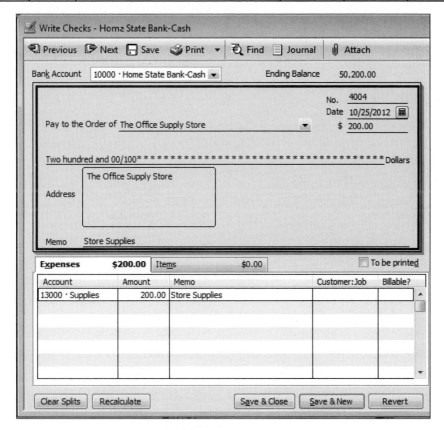

3. When satisfied, click ⌷Save & Close⌷.

4. When Recording Transaction window appears asking if you want to record your changes? Select ⌷ Yes ⌷.

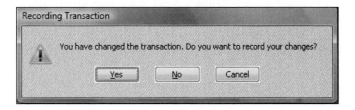

5. You are returned to the Check Register. Notice Home State Bank-Cash balance is now $50,300.00.

6. Close the Check Register.

7. To view the audit trail of this edit, from the Menu Bar select Reports; Accountant & Taxes, Audit Trail (Dates: All). Notice edited check 4003 is not in bold and its State is labeled Prior, meaning it has been replaced.

8. Close the Audit Trail, click [X]. Do not memorize the report.

Write Check for Dividends

Follow these steps to record the payment of a cash dividend to the sole stockholder, Your Name. Your register states:

4005	10/30	Your Name (Acct. No. 30200 Dividends)	200.00		50,100.00

1. From the Home page, click on the icon, Write Checks.

2. The Write Checks window appears. In the Bank Account field, Account No. 10000, Home State Bank appears. Observe that the Ending Balance field shows $50,300, the same as the checkbook register.

3. The To be printed box should be unchecked.

4. Type **4005** in the No. field.

5. Type **10/30/20XX (use your current year)** in the Date field.

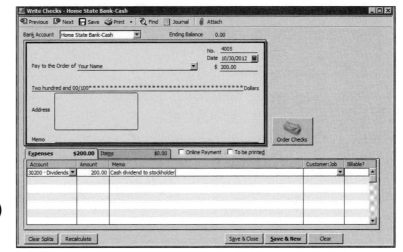

6. Type **200** in the Amount field.

7. In the Pay to field, type **Your Name**. Press <Tab>.

8. In the Items and expenses table, Expenses should be selected. In the first column select Account No. 30200, Dividends.

9. In Memo field type **Cash dividend to stockholder.** Compare your screen to the one shown. When satisfied, click **Save & Close**. You are returned to the Home page.

BACKUP THE OCTOBER CHECK REGISTER

Before you complete account reconciliation, back up your data.

1. From Menu bar, select File; Create Backup.

2. Create a local backup and click **Next**.

3. Pick "Save it now" and click **Next**.

4. Browse to your USB drive to Your Name Chapter 3 folder and name file **Your Name Chapter 3 October Check Register.** Click **Save**.

5. When the window prompts, QuickBooks has saved a backup of the company file...., click **OK** .

6. Exit QuickBooks 2012 or continue to the next section.

ACCOUNT RECONCILIATION

You receive a bank statement every month for your Home State Bank account (Account No. 10000, Home State Bank-Cash) which shows the checks and deposits that have cleared the bank. The Reconcile icon allows you to reconcile the bank statement. Your bank statement for Home State Bank Account is shown here.

Statement of Account			Your Name Retailers	
Home State Bank			Your address	
October 1 to October 31 Account # 89123631			Reno, NV	
REGULAR HOME STATE BANK				
Previous Balance		$ 50,000.00		
1 Deposits (+)		1,500.00		
2 checks (-)		1,200.00		
Service Charges (-)	10/31	10.00		
Ending Balance	10/31	**$50,290.00**		
DEPOSITS				
	10/4	1,500.00		
CHECKS (Asterisk * indicates break in check number sequence)				
	10/5	4002	1,000.00	
	10/30	4005*	200.00	

Follow these steps to reconcile your bank statement balance to Account No. 10000, Home State Bank-Cash.

1. Go to the Banking section of the Home page, click on the Reconcile icon.

2. The Begin Reconciliation window appears.

3. In the Account field, select **10000, Home State Bank-Cash**.

4. Type **10/31/20XX (use your current year)** in the Statement Date field.

5. Confirm 50,000.00 appears as the Beginning Balance.

6. Type **50290.00** in the Ending Balance field.

7. In Service Charge field, type **10.00** for amount and **10/31/20XX** for Date and select account **60400 Bank Service Charge Expense**.

8. Compare your screen to the Begin Reconciliation window shown here. (*Hint:* Your year may differ, as well as the date in the Interest Earned field.)

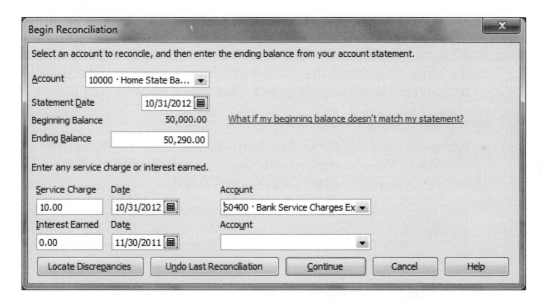

9. Click ⌊ **Continue** ⌋. The Reconcile – Home State Bank-Cash window appears.

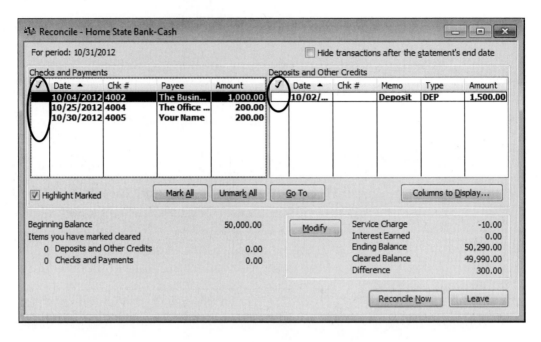

10. Click on the box next to the checks and deposits that have cleared the bank. Make sure the checks that have *not* cleared the bank remain unchecked; for example, Check No. 4004 should *not* be checked.

11. Compare your Reconcile Account – Home State Bank-Cash window to the one shown here. Notice the Difference is 0.00. (*HINT:* Only Reconcile if Difference is 0.00!)

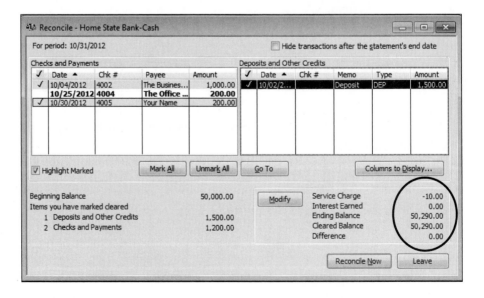

12. Click Reconcile Now. (Select OK or Yes to any messages.) The Select Reconciliation Report window appears. Select to display both the summary and detail reports.

13. Click Display. (Select OK or Yes to any messages.) The Reconciliation Summary report appears. Compare your Reconciliation Summary report to the one shown here.

Select Reconciliation Report

Congratulations! Your account is balanced. All marked items have been cleared in the account register.

Select the type of reconciliation report you'd like to see.

- Summary
- Detail
- ○ Both

To view this report at a later time, select the Report menu, display Banking and then Previous Reconciliation.

Display   Print...   Close

Reconciliation Summary

Customize Report | Share Template | Memorize | Print | E-mail ▾ | Excel ▾ | Hide Header | Collapse | Refresh

2:38 AM
12/20/11

Your Name Retailers Inc.
Reconciliation Summary
10000 · Home State Bank-Cash, Period Ending 10/31/2012

	Oct 31, 12
Beginning Balance	50,000.00
Cleared Transactions	
Checks and Payments - 3 items	-1,210.00
Deposits and Credits - 1 item	1,500.00
Total Cleared Transactions	290.00
Cleared Balance	50,290.00
Uncleared Transactions	
Checks and Payments - 1 item	-200.00
Total Uncleared Transactions	-200.00
Register Balance as of 10/31/2012	50,090.00
Ending Balance	50,090.00

14. Close the Reconciliation Summary and the Reconciliation Detail Report appears. Compare yours to the one shown here.

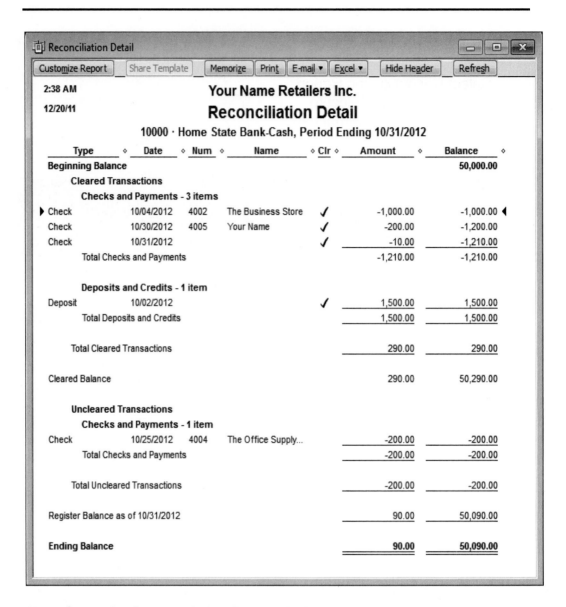

15.   Close the Reconciliation Detail window.

You have successfully completed your transactions for October. Now let's look at how these transactions were debited and credited.

PRINTING THE JOURNAL

To see the journal, follow these steps.

1. From the Navigation Bar, click 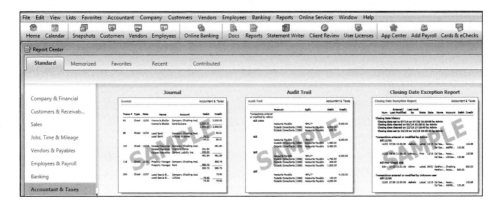 ; Accountant & Taxes. Wait while it opens.

2. Scroll down selections, and click on Journal and customize it.

3. Customize the Journal.

    a. Select Custom from the Dates pulldown menu.
    b. Select **09/30/20XX (use your current year)** in the From field.
    c. Select **10/31/20XX (use your current year)** in the To field.

    d. Click [→] to run the report. If a message appears, click **OK**.

4. The first six transactions are the beginning balances that you entered from the October 1 balance sheet earlier in the chapter.

Scroll down the Transaction Detail report to see all of it. Notice the edited transaction does not appear.

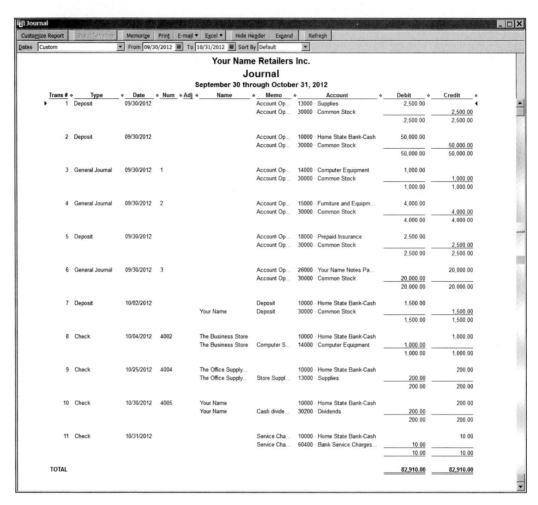

5. Close the Journal report 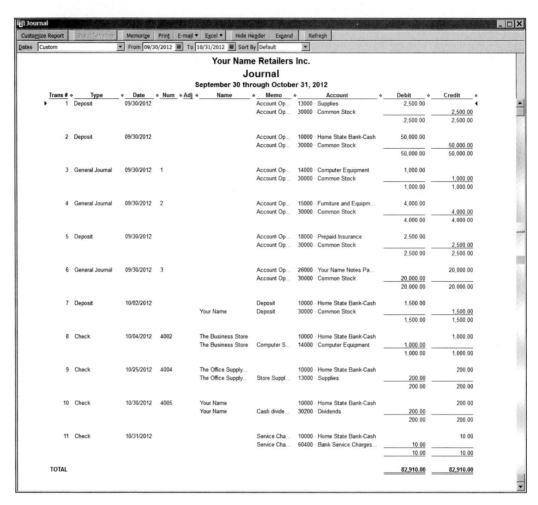 without saving or memorizing.

TRANSACTION DETAIL BY ACCOUNT

Transaction Detail by Account report is similar to a general ledger (GL). For purposes of seeing each account balance, follow the steps below to display the Transaction Detail by Account report.

1. From the Navigation Bar,

    click Reports; Accountant & Taxes, Transaction Detail by Account.

2. Customize the Transaction Detail by Account report (09/30/2012 to 10/31/2012)

    and click ⊕ to run it.

3. The Transaction Detail by Account report displays. Scroll down the window to see the entire report.

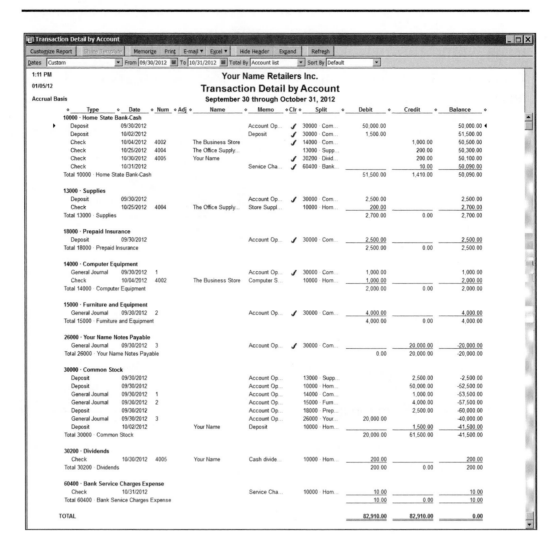

4. Close the Transaction Detail by Account report without saving or memorizing.

TRIAL BALANCE

To display Your Name Retailers' trial balance follow these steps.

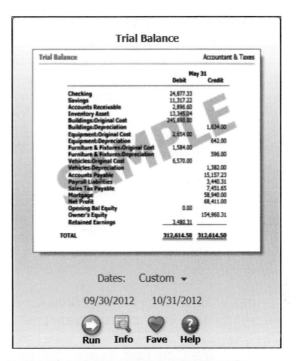

1. From the Navigation Bar, click
 Reports ; Accountant & Taxes, Trial Balance.

2. Customize the Trial Balance report and click ⊙ to run it.

3. Compare your Trial Balance with the one shown.

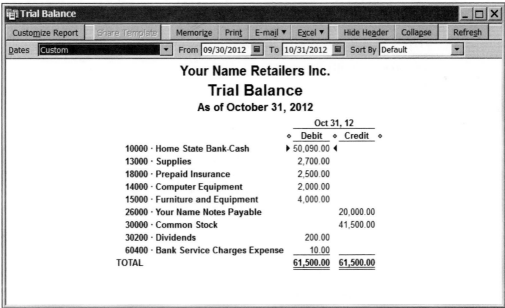

		Oct 31, 12	
		Debit	Credit
10000 · Home State Bank-Cash		50,090.00	
13000 · Supplies		2,700.00	
18000 · Prepaid Insurance		2,500.00	
14000 · Computer Equipment		2,000.00	
15000 · Furniture and Equipment		4,000.00	
26000 · Your Name Notes Payable			20,000.00
30000 · Common Stock			41,500.00
30200 · Dividends		200.00	
60400 · Bank Service Charges Expense		10.00	
TOTAL		61,500.00	61,500.00

4. Close the Trial Balance without saving or memorizing.

FINANCIAL STATEMENTS

To display Your Name Retailers' balance sheet follow these steps.

1. From the Navigation Bar, click Reports ; Company & Financials.

2. From the Profit & Loss (income statement) section, select Profit & Loss Standard.

3. Customize by typing **10/1/20XX to 10/31/20XX (use your current year)** in the Date field. Press ⬀ to run the report.

4. Compare your profit and loss report with the one shown here.

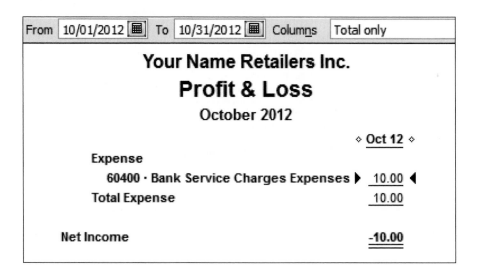

5. Close the profit and loss without saving or memorizing.

6.   From the Navigation Bar, click 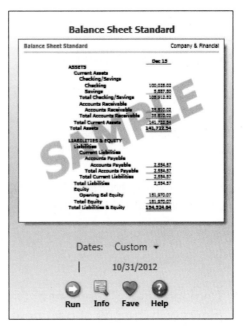; Company & Financials. Scroll down to the Balance Sheet & Net Worth options, select Balance Sheet Standard.

7.   Customize by typing **10/31/20XX (use your current year)** in the Date field. Press ⊙ to run the report.

8.   Compare your Balance Sheet with the one shown.

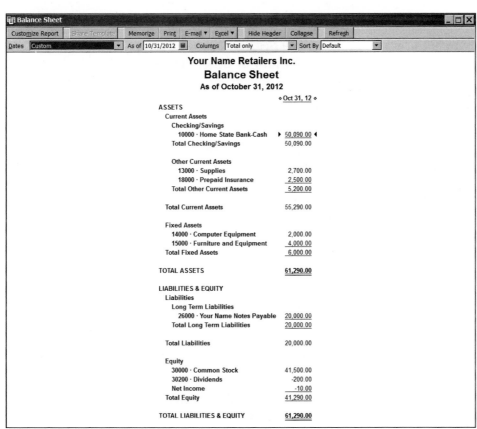

9. Close the balance sheet without saving or memorizing.

10. From the Navigation Bar, click ; Company & Financials. Scroll down to the Cash Flow options, select Statement of Cash Flows.

11. Customize by typing **10/01/20XX** and **10/31/20XX (use your current year)** in the Date fields. Press to run the report.

12. Compare your Statement of Cash Flows with the one shown here.

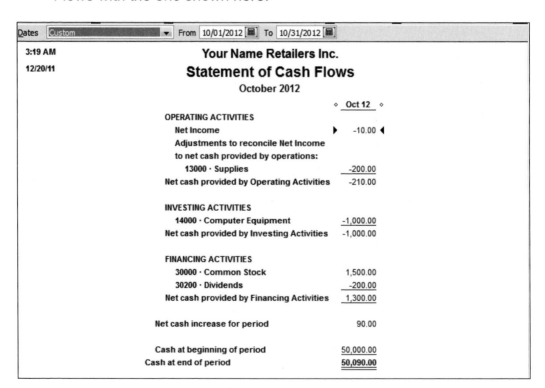

	Oct 12
OPERATING ACTIVITIES	
Net Income	▶ -10.00 ◀
Adjustments to reconcile Net Income to net cash provided by operations:	
13000 · Supplies	-200.00
Net cash provided by Operating Activities	-210.00
INVESTING ACTIVITIES	
14000 · Computer Equipment	-1,000.00
Net cash provided by Investing Activities	-1,000.00
FINANCING ACTIVITIES	
30000 · Common Stock	1,500.00
30200 · Dividends	-200.00
Net cash provided by Financing Activities	1,300.00
Net cash increase for period	90.00
Cash at beginning of period	50,000.00
Cash at end of period	50,090.00

Your Name Retailers Inc.
Statement of Cash Flows
October 2012

3:19 AM
12/20/11

13. Close the cash flow statement without saving or memorizing.

BACKUP CHAPTER 3 DATA

Before going on to the end of chapter exercises, follow these steps to backup Chapter 3 data.

1. From Menu bar, select File; Create Backup.

2. Create a local backup and click [**Next**].

3. Pick "Save it now" and click [**Next**].

4. Browse to your USB drive to Your Name Chapter 3 folder and name file **Your Name Chapter 3 October End.** Click [Save].

5. When the window prompts, QuickBooks has saved a backup of the company file…., click [**OK**].

6. Exit QuickBooks 2012 or continue to the next section.

SUMMARY AND REVIEW

OBJECTIVES: In Chapter 3, you used the software to:

1.   Open company called Your Name Retailers Inc.
2.   Set preferences.
3.   Edit the chart of accounts.
4.   Enter beginning balances.
5.   Record check register entries.
6.   Edit to correct an error.
7.   Complete account reconciliation.
8.   Display the trial balance.
9.   Display the financial statements.
10. Make backup of work.[2]

---

[2]The chart in the Preface shows you the size of each backup file. Refer to this chart for backing up data. Remember, you can back up to a hard drive location or external media.

Additional textbook related resources are on the textbook website at www.mhhe.com/QBessentials2012. It includes chapter resources, including troubleshooting tips, online quizzes, etc.

RESOURCEFUL QUICKBOOKS

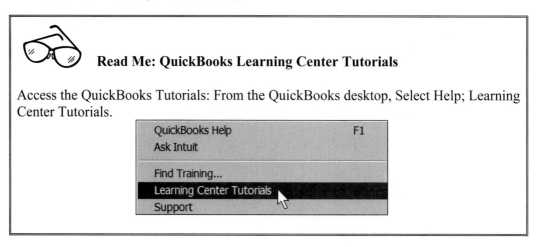

View the QuickBooks Learning Center video tutorials about "Reports" and "Adding and Using QuickBooks Accounts" then answer the following questions.

1. What does memorizing a report do?

2. What is QuickZoom?

3. In the Adding and Using QuickBooks Accounts video, what account did you set up and use?

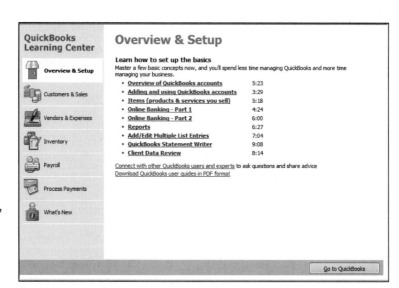

Multiple Choice Questions: The Online Learning Center includes the multiple-choice questions at www.mhhe.com/QBessentials2012, select Student Edition, Chapter 3, Multiple Choice.

_____1. How many backups were made of company data in Chapter 3?

    a. One.
    b. Two.
    c. Three.
    d. Four.

_____2. The Business Store is a:

    a. Vendor.
    b. Customer.
    c. Employee.
    d. Other.

_____3. The Home page area that includes write checks is:

    a. Employees.
    b. Vendors.
    c. Banking.
    d. Company.

_____4. An Audit Trail report shows:

    a. All transactions.
    b. Only edited transactions.
    c. Only voided transactions.
    d. Only duplicate transactions.

_____5. How often should an account be reconciled?

    a. Daily.
    b. Weekly.
    c. Monthly.
    d. Quarterly.

_____6. Reconciliation reports generated when an account is reconcile include:

   a. Summary.
   b. Detail.
   c. Both.
   d. No report is generated.

_____7. In Report Center under Accountant & Taxes, all of the following reports can be generated except:

   a. Transaction Detail by Account.
   b. Transaction List by Date.
   c. Audit Trail.
   d. Unclassified.

_____8. In the Report Center under Company & Financial all of the following reports can be found for Profit & Loss except:

   a. Prev Year Comparison.
   b. By Job.
   c. By Class.
   d. By Date.

_____9. In the Report Center under Company & Financial all of the following reports can be found for Balance Sheet & Net Worth except:

   a. Summary.
   b. YTD Comparison.
   c. Prev Year Comparison.
   d. Net Worth Graph.

_____10. In the Report Center under Company & Financial all of the following reports can be found for Cash Flow Report except:

   a. Statement of Cash Flows.
   b. Cash Flow Forecast.
   c. All of the above.
   d. None of the above.

True/Make True: To answer these questions, go online to www.mhhe.com/QBessentials2012, link to Student Edition, Chapter 3, QA Templates. The analysis question is also included.

1.   In Chapter 3, the checkbook register and September 30, 20XX balance sheet are used as source documents.

2.   In accounting, written evidence of a business transaction is called an account register.

3.   Two actions are necessary when a company writes a check in error, the check must be voided and the entry must be edited in QuickBooks.

4.   Two backups were made in Chapter 3 of Your Name Retailers Inc. company data.

5.   The first date for recording transactions is 10/01/20XX.

6.   The company preference for write checks and record deposits is Account No. 10000, Home State Bank.

7.   The total cash balance on 10/31/20XX is $50,000.00.

8.   The 10/31/20XX Income Statement for Your Name Retailers Inc. had a net income.

9.   The total assets on the 10/31/20XX Balance Sheet for Your Name Retailers Inc. were $100,000.00.

10.   Your Name Retailers Inc. had a positive cash flow for the month of October.

Exercise 3-1: Follow the instructions to complete Exercise 3-1. You must complete Chapter 3 activities *before* you can do Exercise 3-1.

1. Print the Chart of Accounts. (Refer to the Read me box for saving reports as PDF files.)

2. Print the 9/30/20XX to 10/31/20XX journal.

3. Print the 9/30/20XX to 10/31/20XX transaction detail by account.

Exercise 3-2: Follow the instructions below to complete Exercise 3-2.

1. Print the 9/30/20XX to 10/31/20XX trial balance.

2. Print the 10/01/20XX to 10/31/20XX profit and loss report.

3. Print the 10/31/20XX balance sheet.

4. Print the 10/01/20XX to 10/31/20XX cash flow statement.

 Read Me: Save QB reports as PDF Files

Your instructor may want you to email the QB reports as PDF attachments. To do that, follow these steps:

1. Display the report.
2. From the menu bar, select File; Save as PDF. *Or,* click the report's E-mail button and select Send reports as PDF.
3. The suggested file name is **Exercise 3-1 Chart of Accounts.pdf**, etc.

You need Adobe Reader to save as PDF files. If download the free Adobe Reader, www.adobe.com.

Analysis Question: Why are the trial balance totals different from the balance sheet totals?

Chapter 4

Working with Inventory, Vendors, and Customers

OBJECTIVES:

1. Open the company, Your Name Retailers Inc.
2. Enter items and inventory preferences.
3. Enter vendor records.
4. Enter inventory items.
5. Print the vendor list and item list.
6. Enter bills and record purchase returns.
7. Pay bills.
8. Add a vendor and non-inventory item on the fly.
9. Enter customer records and defaults.
10. Record customer sales on account and sales returns.
11. Receive customer payments.
12. Make backups.[1]

Additional textbook resources are on the textbook website at www.mhhe.com/QBessentials2012 including chapter resources, online quizzes, etc.

GETTING STARTED

Your Name Retailers Inc. started operations on October 1, 20XX (use your current year) in Reno, NV and is organized as a corporation. Customers purchase three products from Your Name Retailers Inc. The three products sold by Your Name Retailers are:

 ➢ Podcasts (audio files).
 ➢ ebooks (PDF files). PDF is an abbreviation of portable document format.
 ➢ TV programs (video files).

---

[1]The chart in the Preface, page xii, shows the file name and size of each backup file. Refer to this chart for backing up data. Remember, you can back up to a hard drive location or external media.

Follow these steps to open Your Name Retailers Inc.

1. Start QuickBooks by clicking on the icon on your desktop. You should see Your Name Retailers Inc. on the title bar.

   Your Name Retailers Inc. - QuickBooks Accountant 2012.

2. If you do <u>not</u> see Your Name Retailers Inc. on the title bar, follow these steps.

   a. Select File; Close Company. In the No Company Open pane, click on Open or restore an existing company button.

   b. In Open or Restore window, select Restore a backup copy. Click Next.

   c. Select Local backup. Click Next.

   d. Browse your external media and select the Your Name Chapter 3 October End.QBB backup that you made in the Chapter 3. (This backup was made on page 101.) Click Open.

   e. In the Where do you want to restore the file? window, click Next. The Save Company File as window appears.

   f. Rename Your Name Retailers Inc.Chapter 3.qbw to **Your Name Chapter 4 October Begin**. Observe that the Save as type field shows QuickBooks Files (*.QBW). Click Save. The title bar shows Your Name Retailers Inc. - QuickBooks Accountant 2012.

   g. When the QuickBooks Information window prompts Your data has been restored successfully, click OK.

   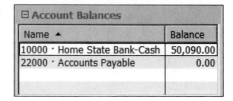

3. On your QuickBooks desktop notice the cash balance in the Home State Bank-Cash account is $50,090.00.

⊟ Account Balances	
Name ▲	Balance
10000 · Home State Bank-Cash	50,090.00
22000 · Accounts Payable	0.00

4.   To confirm that you are starting in the correct place, display the

10/31 trial balance. (*HINT:* From the Navigation Bar, select 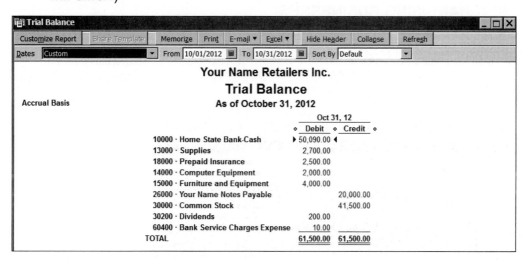 **Reports** ;
Accountant & Taxes, Trial Balance.)

5.   Compare your trial balance with the one shown below. (Your year
will differ.)

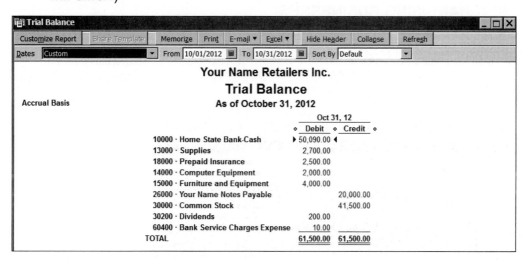

6.   Close the trial balance.

ITEMS & INVENTORY PREFERENCES

Follow these steps to set preferences for items and inventory.

1.   From the menu bar,
select Edit;
Preferences.

2.   Select Items &
Inventory, then
select the Company
Preferences tab.

3.   Click on the box next
to Inventory and
purchase orders are
active to place a
checkmark in the
box.

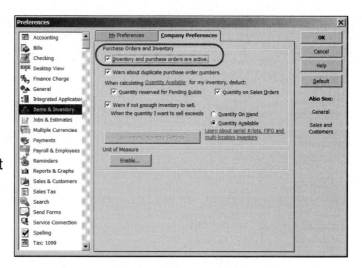

4.   Click [**OK**]. When the Warning window prompts, QuickBooks must close all its open windows to change this preference, click [**OK**].

5.   Click [Home] to return to the QB desktop.

MERCHANDISING BUSINESSES

Merchandising businesses purchase the merchandise they sell from suppliers known as *vendors*. A vendor is a person or company from whom Your Name Retailers buys products or services. When Your Name Retailers makes a purchase on account from vendors, the transaction is known as an *accounts payable transaction*. Purchases made on account involve payment terms; for example, Your Name Retailers purchases inventory on account from a vendor. The vendor offers the Your Name Retailers 30 days to pay for the purchase. This is shown as Net 30 in the Payment terms field of the vendor record

QuickBooks organizes and monitors Your Name Retailers' *accounts payable*. Accounts Payable is a group of accounts that show the amounts owed to vendors or creditors for goods, supplies, or services purchased on account.

When entering a purchase, you select the vendor's name and item. The vendor's address information, payment terms, and appropriate accounts are automatically debited and credited. This works similarly for accounts receivable.

The Vendors section of the Home page illustrates the work flow of entering and paying a vendor bill as well as the tracking of any inventory items purchased on account.

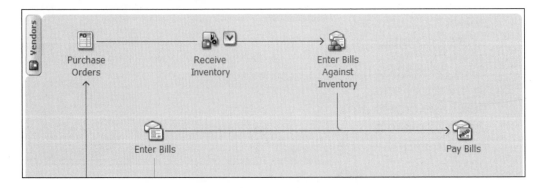

VENDORS

On the Vendors Center desktop, you perform all the tasks related to vendors and payables. QuickBooks maintains vendor records and tracks their contact information and financial details and history. The Vendors Center is the starting point for managing vendor purchases and the tracking of inventory items purchased.

The next section shows you how to set up vendors. Follow these steps to enter vendor default information.

1. On the Navigation Bar, select .

2. On Task Bar, select New Vendor; New Vendor. If a window pops up about new features, read and click [OK]. The New Vendor window appears.

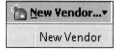

Complete the following fields:

Vendor Name:	**Podcast Ltd.**
Opening Balance:	**0** as of **10/01/20XX** (use your current year)
Company Name:	**Podcast Ltd.**
First Name:	**Howie**
Last Name:	**Hansen**
Phone:	**213-555-0100**
FAX:	**213-555-0300**
Alt. Contact:	**Delores Duke**

E-mail: **howie@podcast.net**
Print on Check as: **Podcast Ltd.**

In the Addresses, Billed From Address field, type the following:
1341 Barrington Road
Los Gatos, CA 90046 USA

Compare your New Vendor window to the one shown here.

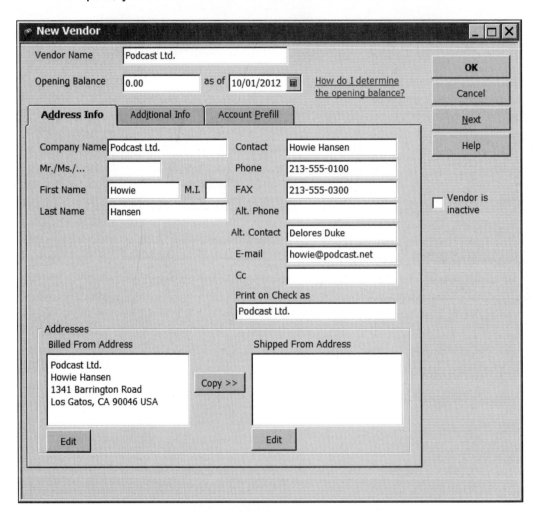

3. Click on the Additional Info tab. Complete the following fields:

    Account No.:   **22000**
    Type: **Suppliers**
    Terms: **Net 30**

Credit limit: **10,000.00**

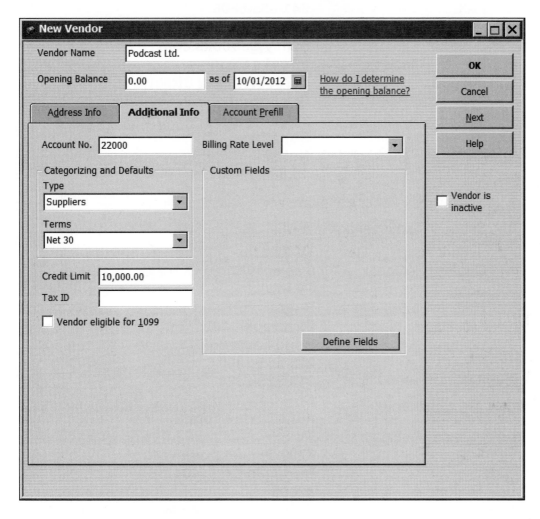

4.   Click on the Account Prefill tab. Leave blank.

5.   Review data under each tab, when satisfied, click   Next   .

6.   Set up the next vendor record:

Vendor Name: **eBooks Express**
Opening Balance: **0** as of **10/01/20XX** (use your current year)
Company Name: **eBooks Express**
First Name: **Nancy**
Last Name: **Noel**
Contact: **Nancy Noel**

Phone:	**541-555-4320**
FAX:	**541-555-8808**
Alt. Contact:	**Abby Angel**
E-mail:	**nancy@ebooks.com**
Print on Check as:	**eBooks Express**
Address:	**10756 NW First Street**
	Gig Harbor, OR 97330 USA
Account:	**22000**
Type:	**Suppliers**
Terms:	**Net 30**
Credit limit:	**10,000.00**

7.   Review data under each tab, when satisfied, click [Next].

8.   Set up the next vendor record.

Vendor Name:	**TV Flix**
Opening Balance:	**0** as of **10/01/20XX** (use your current year)
Company Name:	**TV Flix**
First Name:	**Hugo**
Last Name:	**Saybrook**
Contact:	**Hugo Saybrook**
Phone:	**213-555-1690**
FAX:	**213-555-6320**
Alt. Contact:	**Cori Columbo**
E-mail:	**hugo@tvflix.com**
Print on Check as:	**TV Flix**
Address:	**7709 Sunset Boulevard**
	Burbank, CA 91501 USA
Account:	**22000**
Type:	**Suppliers**
Terms:	**Net 30**
Credit limit:	**10,000.00**

9.   Click [OK] to return to the Vendor Center Home page.

10. Notice all of your vendors, the three you added this chapter plus the two you added previously when you purchased supplies and furniture (Chapter 3) are listed in the left pane of the Vendor Center window with account balances of zero.

Vendors	Transactions

View Active Vendors ▼

Find [   ] 🔍

Name	Balance Total
eBooks Express	0.00
Podcast Ltd.	0.00
The Business Store	0.00
The Office Supply Store	0.00
TV Flix	0.00

INVENTORY ITEMS

An *inventory item* is a product that is purchased for sale and is tracked in Account No. 12100, Inventory, on the balance sheet. Because the Inventory account is increased or decreased for every purchase, sale or return, its balance in the general ledger is current. In QuickBooks when you purchase and receive inventory items, they are added to inventory. When you sell these items and they are added to an invoice, the items are subtracted from inventory.

Complete the following steps to add a new item to inventory.

1. If necessary, close the Vendor Center. From the Home page, select ![Inventory Activities], Inventory Center. From the Inventory Center, select ![New Inventory Item... ▼], New Inventory Item. Read, then close the New Feature window by clicking [OK].

2. In the New Item window in the Type field, select Inventory Part from the pulldown menu. The New Item window changes and appears as follows:

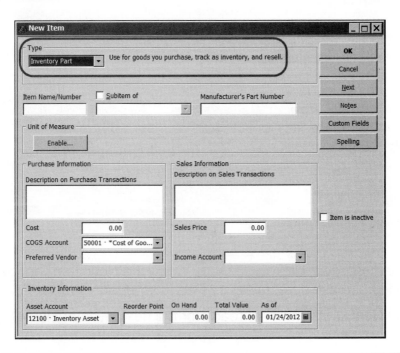

3. Complete these fields:

    Item Name/Number: **Podcast**
    Description on Purchase Transactions and Sales Transactions:
                         audio files (Sales automatically fills)
    Cost: **15.00**
    COGS Account: **Account No. 50001, Cost of Goods Sold**
    Preferred Vendor: **Podcast Ltd.**
    Sales Price: **30.00**
    Income Account: **Account No. 46000, Sales**
    Inventory Account: **12100, Inventory Asset**
    On Hand: 0.00
    Total Value: 0.00
    As of: **10/01/20XX** (use your current year)

4. Compare your New Item window to the one below.

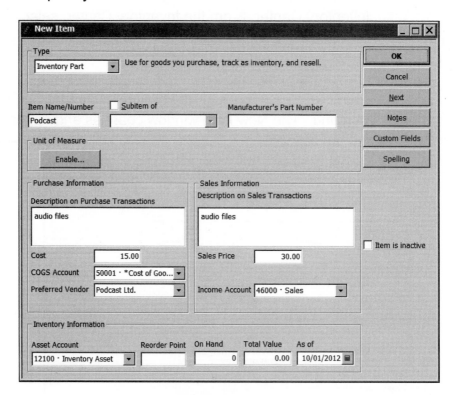

5. When satisfied, click [Next]. When the New Item window appears, make sure Inventory Part is selected.

6. The New Item window is ready for the next inventory item.

Complete the fields shown here.

Item Name/Number: **eBook**
Description on Purchase Transactions and Sales Transactions:
    PDF files
Cost: **25.00**
COGS Account: Account No. 50001, Cost of Goods Sold

Preferred Vendor: **eBooks Express**
Sales Price: **50.00**
Income Account: Account No. 46000, Sales
Inventory Account: Account No. 12100, Inventory Asset
On Hand: 0.00
Total Value: 0.00
As of: **10/01/20XX** (use your current year)

7.   Click [Next] when satisfied.

8.   If Check Spelling on Form window appears checking the spelling of PDF, select [Ignore All].

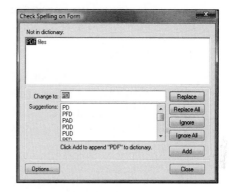

9.   The New Item window is ready for the next inventory part. Complete the fields shown here.

Item Name/Number: **TV Programs**
Description on Purchase Transactions and Sales Transactions:
    video files
Cost: 30.00
COGS Account: Account No.50001, Cost of Goods Sold
Preferred Vendor: TV Flix
Sales Price: 60.00
Income Account: Account No. 46000, Sales
Inventory Account: Account No. 12100, Inventory Asset
On Hand: 0.00
Total Value   0.00
As of: 10/01/20XX (use your current year)

10.   When satisfied, click to return to the Vendor Center.

LISTS

You just added three vendors and three inventory items. QuickBooks' list feature shows the details of each record.

Vendor List

The vendor list shows information about the vendors with whom you do business. Follow these steps to display the vendor list.

1. From the Navigation Bar, select [Vendors]; click on Vendor tab in the left pane. The Vendor List appears. Observe you can view list by All Vendors, Active Vendors, Vendors with Open Balances, or Custom Filter.

2. To see The Business Store vendor record, drill down. (*Hint:* Double-click on The Business Store vendor. If a window pops up about new features, click [OK].)

3. Since this vendor was added on the fly in the previous chapter, you need to add vendor information. The Business Store is located at 1234 Front Range Road, Reno, NV 89555; telephone 775-555-1234; e-mail: jimmy@tbs.com, and contact is Jimmy T.; Additional information includes Account No. 22000, Type: Suppliers, Terms:

    Net 30, and Credit limit: $5,000. Click [OK] to return to the Vendors List.

4. To see The Office Supply Store vendor record, drill down. Add the following vendor information: The Office Supply Store is located at 9876 Hogback Road, Reno, NV 89555; telephone 775-555-9876; e-mail: sophie@oss.com; and contact is Sophie W. Additional information includes Account No. 22000, Type: Suppliers, Terms:

    Net 30, and Credit limit: $5,000. Click [OK] to return to the Vendors List.

5. Click on the [→|] button at the top of the Vendor list to show the full list only.

6. Click on the [|←] button at the top right of the Vendor list to show list and details.

Item List

The Item List shows information about inventory items including name, description, type, account, on hand, and price. When you open the list, you view the active items.

Follow the steps on below to display the item list.

1. From the Menu Bar, select Vendors; Items List. The Item List appears. If necessary, double-click on the Name column to list the items in alphabetic order.

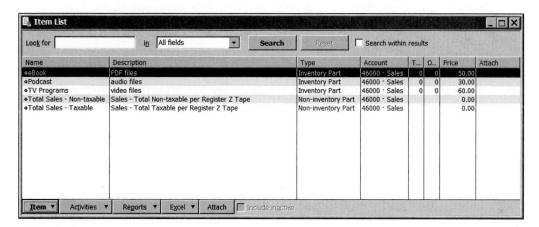

2. Notice there are several items listed that you did not add, Total Sales - Non-taxable and Total Sales - Taxable.

3. Since Your Name Retailers Inc. is located in Nevada, there is no sales tax.

4. To delete Total Sales - Non-Taxable, highlight it. Use the Item pulldown menu to select Delete Item. When asked "Are you sure you want to delete this item?" Select OK .

5. Delete Total Sales - Taxable, too.

6. Now the three items you added appear in the list.

7. To see an item record, drill-down by double-clicking on it.

8. Click on ⊠ to return to the Vendor Center.

9. Close all Windows. (*HINT:* Select Window, Close all. Then, click 🏠 Home .)

10. Backup if you are working in a computer lab to your USB drive or continue to the next section. The suggested file name is **Your Name Chapter 4 Vendors and Inventory.**

VENDOR TRANSACTIONS

In the Vendors section of the Home page, you perform all the tasks related to vendors and payables. It is the starting point for managing vendor purchases and inventory. In this section, you work with some of these features.

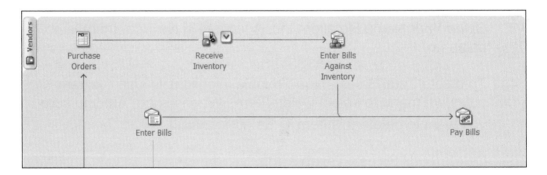

In the Vendor pane of the Home page, notice you can enter purchase orders placed with vendors, receive inventory, enter bills received against inventory, enter bills, and pay bills.

Vendor and Payable Reports

In the Reports Center (Navigation Bar; 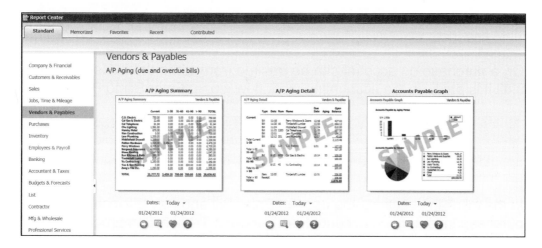Reports), there are many vendors and payables reports, including those that focus on A/P Aging, Vendor Balances, Lists, and related reports. In this chapter you will use them to gain quick access to vendor or payable information.

A/P Aging (due and overdue bills)

Vendor Balances

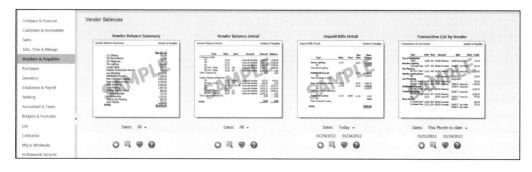

Accounts Payable Tasks

In QuickBooks, all information about a purchase is recorded in the Vendors pane of the Home page. Then, QuickBooks takes the necessary information from the Vendors pane and automatically does the accounting debits and credits.

There are two ways to make a purchase on account in QuickBooks. You can use a purchase order tracking system where a purchase is followed from its initial request until payment. In the accounting work flow icons: Purchase Order to Receive Inventory to Enter Bills Against Inventory to Pay Bills. (To illustrate, the work flow was altered slightly.)

Or, a purchase on account can be tracked from when the bill is received until it is paid. In the accounting work flow icons: Enter Bill to Pay Bill.

In the following section, you use the Enter Bill and Pay Bill icons to purchase inventory on account from vendors. Transaction processing is dependent on which defaults are set for vendors and inventory items. Since vendor defaults were set up earlier in this chapter this means that vendor information is completed automatically in the Enter Bills window. Purchases from vendors are posted to both the General Ledger and to detailed vendors and payables accounts. In accounting, vendors and payables details are shown in the **accounts payable ledger**.

When Your Name Retailers pays vendors, QuickBooks' Pay Bills feature is used. Purchases work hand in hand with payments. Once you have entered a bill, it is available when you pay bills. Then, QuickBooks distributes the appropriate amounts.

The next section explains how to enter bills. The term bill and invoice are used interchangeably. A **bill** or **invoice** is a request for payment for products or services.

Enter Bills

The transaction you are going to record is:

Date   *Description of Transaction*

11/02   Invoice No. 5 received from Podcast Ltd. for the purchase
             of 20 audio files, $15 each, for a total of $300.

Follow these steps to record this transaction.

1.   From the Vendor Pane on the Home page,
     select the Enter Bills icon.

2.   When the Enter Bills window appears, complete the following fields:

     Date: **11/02/20XX (use your current year)**
                              (Press <Tab> between fields)
     Vendor: Podcast Ltd.
     Memo: Invoice No. 5

     Click on Items Tab, complete the following fields:

     Item: Podcast
     Description: audio files is completed automatically
     Qty: **20**
     Cost: 15.00 is completed automatically
     Amount: 300.00 is completed automatically

     Compare your Enter Bills window to the one shown on the next
     page.

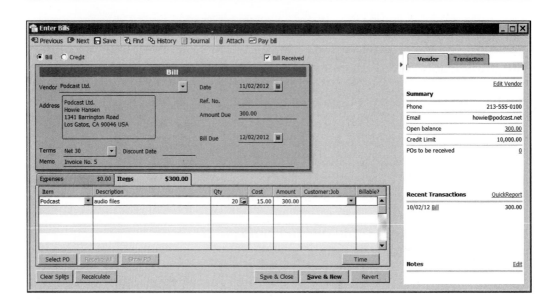

3. Click [Save & Close]. Before completing the next transaction, let's see how QuickBooks debited and credited this information.

4. From the Navigation Bar, select

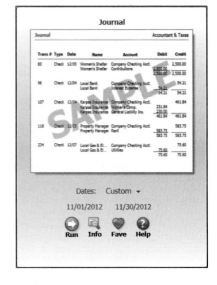

 [Reports]; Accountant & Taxes, Journal. Select Custom for Dates. Type **11/01/20XX** (your current year) in the From field and **11/02/20XX** (your current year) in the To field. Click Run to display the report.

5. The transaction was debited and credited as follows:

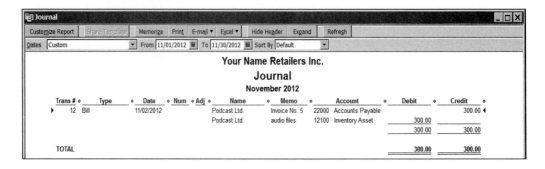

When the 12100 Inventory account is debited, it is increased. When the 22000 Accounts Payable account is credited it is also increased. Your Name Retailers owes Podcast Ltd. $300 for this purchase. Close the Journal without saving.

6.   To see how this transaction is recorded in the accounts payable ledger, go to the Vendor Center Home page.

7.   In Vendor pane on left side of window, click on Podcast Ltd.

8.   In right pane in the Show field, All Transactions should be displayed. The Bill for Podcast Ltd. appears. The Vendor Transaction History can be substituted for the accounts payable ledger.

9.   Double click on the Bill to view the Enter Bill source document. Close the Enter Bills window.

10.   Enter the following bills. (*HINT:* From the Vendor Pane on the Home page, select the Enter Bills icon.) Remember to click Save & New after each transaction. Saving posts the transaction to the appropriate accounts in the general ledger and accounts payable ledger.

Date	*Description of Transaction*
11/03	Invoice No. 90eB received from eBooks Express for the purchase of 15 PDF files, $25 each, for a total of $375. (*Hint:* In the Item field, select eBook.)
11/03	Invoice No. 210TV received from TV Flix for the purchase of 25 video files, $30 each, for a total of $750. (*Hint:* In the Item field, select TV Programs.)
11/05	Invoice No. 78PS received from Podcast Ltd. for the purchase of 18 audio files, $15 each, for a total of $270.

Purchase Returns

Sometimes it is necessary to return merchandise that has been purchased from a vendor. When entering a purchase return, you need to record it as a Credit instead of a Bill in the Enter Bills window.

The following transaction is for merchandise returned to a vendor.

Date	*Description of Transaction*
11/10	Returned two video files to TV Flix from Invoice No. 210TV, Credit Memo No. CM1, for a total of $60.

Follow these steps to record a credit memo.

1. If Enter Bills window is displayed, click on the Enter Bills icon found on the Home page.

2. When the Enter Bills window appears, select the Credit radio button and complete the following fields:

Date:	**11/10/20XX (use your current year)**
Vendor:	TV Flix
Ref. No.	**CM1**
Memo:	**Invoice No. 210TV**
Item:	TV Programs
Qty:	**2**

3. Compare your Enter Bills, Credit window to the one shown on next page.

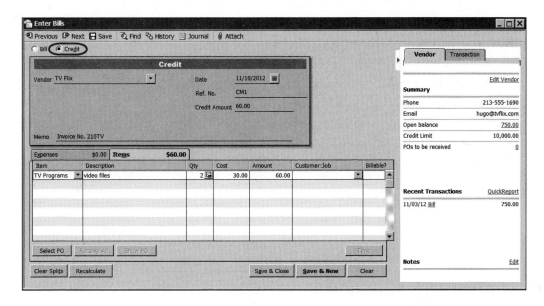

4.   After comparing your Enter Bills; Credit window click [S̲a̲ve & Close]

5.   Let's see how this entry is journalized. Go to Report Center;
     Accountant & Taxes, Journal, date is 11/10/20XX. Observe that
     22000 Accounts Payable TV Flix is debited for $60. This reduces
     the accounts payable account balance by $60. Also, 12100
     Inventory is credited for $60. This reduces the inventory account
     balance by the amount of the return. After viewing, close Journal
     without saving it.

6.   To see how the accounts payable ledger records this transaction,
     display the Vendor Center. In Vendors tab, highlight TV Flix. In
     right pane, make sure Show All Transactions is displayed. Observe
     that the balance in the TV Flix account is reduced by $60 on
     11/10/20XX.

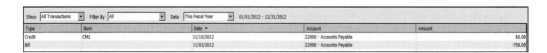

Type	Num	Date ▼	Account	Amount
Credit	CM1	11/10/2012	22000 · Accounts Payable	60.00
Bill		11/03/2012	22000 · Accounts Payable	-750.00

7. To determine the balance in the Accounts Payable account on 11/10/20XX, go to Report Center, Vendors & Payables, Vendor Balance Summary. Select All Dates. Observe that the Total of all Vendor Balances is $1,635.

> **Your Name Retailers Inc.**
> # Vendor Balance Summary
> **All Transactions**
>
> | | ◇ Nov 10, 12 ◇ |
> |---|---|
> | eBooks Express ▶ | 375.00 ◀ |
> | Podcast Ltd. | 570.00 |
> | TV Flix | 690.00 |
> | TOTAL | **1,635.00** |

8. This should agree with the 11/10/20XX Balance Sheet for Accounts Payable. (Report Center;

> **LIABILITIES & EQUITY**
> **Liabilities**
>   **Current Liabilities**
> | Accounts Payable | 1,635.00 |
> |---|---|
> | **Total Current Liabilities** | 1,635.00 |

Company & Financial, Balance Sheet & Net Worth, Balance Sheet Summary. Custom Dates as of 11/10/20XX.) The general ledger balance for accounts payable is 1,635.00. This is the *same* amount that is shown on the Vendor Balance Summary report.

9. Close the Balance Sheet Summary, Report Center, and any other open windows to return to the Home page.

Vendor Payments

Use the Pay Bills icon on the Home page to pay vendor bills. The Pay Bills form will display a list of the company's unpaid bills. You can choose to pay individual bills or pay all of them.

In the transaction that follows, all vendor bills are paid.

Date	*Description of Transaction*
11/20	Your Name Retailers pays all outstanding vendor bills for a total of $1,635.

1. From the Vendors pane on the Home page, click on the Pay Bills icon.

2. When the Enter Bills window appears, select the Show All Bills radio button.

3. Click [Select All Bills].

4. Confirm Method field shows Check.

5. Confirm the Account field shows 10000, Home State Bank-Cash.

6. Type Payment Date, **11/20/20XX** (use your current year).

7. Since Your Name Retailers returned merchandise to TV Flix, highlight TV Flix. The Discount & Credit Information for Highlighted Bill appears. Observe that the Total Credits Available field shows $60.00.

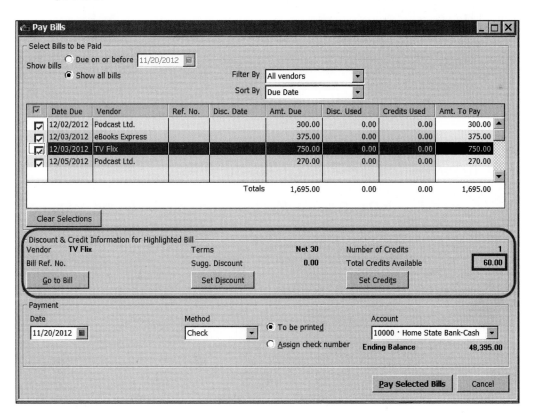

8. Click on [Set Credits].

9. When Discounts and Credits window appears, click [**Done**].

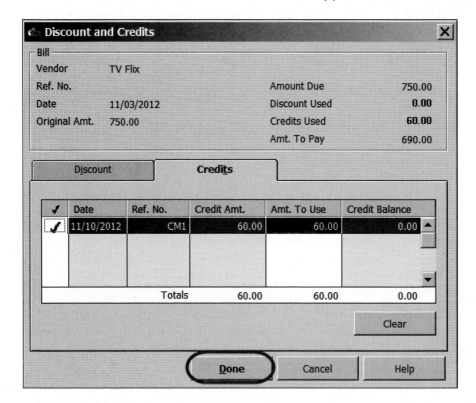

10. Observe that the Credits used for TV Flix shows <u>$60.00</u>; the Amt. To Pay column shows $690 (750 –60 = 690).

11. Compare your Pay Bills window to the one shown on the next page. Observe that the Totals row shows $1,635. This agrees with the accounts payable balance shown on page 128.

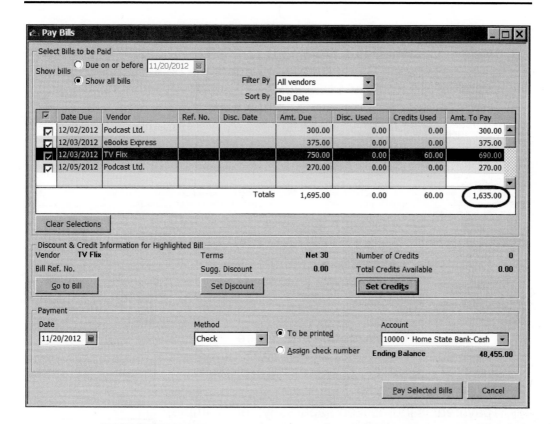

12. Click  Pay Selected Bills .

13. The Payment Summary window appears.

14. Click Done . (*NOTE:* If this were a real business you would have printed and mailed the checks.)

15. Display the detailed account balance for Account No. 22000, Accounts Payable. (Report Center;

Payment Summary

Payment Details
Payment Date   11/20/2012
Payment Account   10000 · Home State Bank-Cash
Payment Method   Check

Payments have been successfully recorded for the following 4 of 4 bills:

Date Due	Vendor	Amount Paid
12/03/2012	eBooks Express	375.00
12/02/2012	Podcast Ltd.	300.00
12/05/2012	Podcast Ltd.	270.00
12/03/2012	TV Flix	690.00
	Total	1,635.00

How do I find and change a bill payment?

You can print checks now or print them later from Print Forms on the File menu.

[Pay More Bills] [Print Checks] [Done]

Company & Financial, Balance Sheet & Net Worth, Balance Sheet Detail. Custom Dates From 10/01/20XX To 11/20/20XX.) Observe that the Balance Sheet Detail shows that the balance in Accounts Payable is 0.00 as of 11/20/20XX. Close report without saving it.

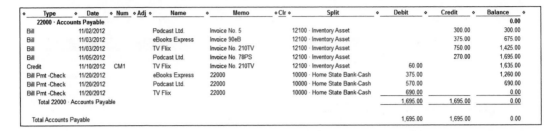

Type	Date	Num	Adj	Name	Memo	Clr	Split	Debit	Credit	Balance
22000 · Accounts Payable										0.00
Bill	11/02/2012			Podcast Ltd.	Invoice No. 5		12100 · Inventory Asset		300.00	300.00
Bill	11/03/2012			eBooks Express	Invoice 90eB		12100 · Inventory Asset		375.00	675.00
Bill	11/03/2012			TV Flix	Invoice No. 210TV		12100 · Inventory Asset		750.00	1,425.00
Bill	11/05/2012			Podcast Ltd.	Invoice No. 78PS		12100 · Inventory Asset		270.00	1,695.00
Credit	11/10/2012	CM1		TV Flix	Invoice No. 210TV		12100 · Inventory Asset	60.00		1,635.00
Bill Pmt -Check	11/20/2012			eBooks Express	22000		10000 · Home State Bank-Cash	375.00		1,260.00
Bill Pmt -Check	11/20/2012			Podcast Ltd.	22000		10000 · Home State Bank-Cash	570.00		690.00
Bill Pmt -Check	11/20/2012			TV Flix	22000		10000 · Home State Bank-Cash	690.00		0.00
Total 22000 · Accounts Payable								1,695.00	1,695.00	0.00
Total Accounts Payable								1,695.00	1,695.00	0.00

16. Display the Vendor Center Vendors tab. Observe that each vendor shows a zero balance.

17. To see how the vendor payments are journalized, display the 11/20/20XX Journal. (Report Center; Accountant & Taxes, Journal, date is 11/20/20XX) Observe that each vendor payment is journalized separately; for example, the November 20th vendor payment to eBooks Express shows a debit to Account No. 22000 for $375; and a credit to Account No. 10000, Home State Bank for $375. If you add the three payments together they equal, $1,635, which is the total of the three payments—375+690+570=1,635.

Your Name Retailers Inc.
Journal
November 20, 2012

Trans #	Type	Date	Num	Adj	Name	Memo	Account	Debit	Credit
17	Bill Pmt -Check	11/20/2012			eBooks Express	22000	10000 · Home State Bank-Cash		375.00
					eBooks Express	22000	22000 · Accounts Payable	375.00	
								375.00	375.00
18	Bill Pmt -Check	11/20/2012			Podcast Ltd.	22000	10000 · Home State Bank-Cash		570.00
					Podcast Ltd.	22000	22000 · Accounts Payable	570.00	
								570.00	570.00
19	Bill Pmt -Check	11/20/2012			TV Flix	22000	10000 · Home State Bank-Cash		690.00
					TV Flix	22000	22000 · Accounts Payable	690.00	
								690.00	690.00
TOTAL								**1,635.00**	**1,635.00**

Purchasing Assets from Vendors

In the previous chapter you purchased assets for cash and used the check register as your source document. Now, along with credit purchases for inventory, assets can also be purchased on account from vendors. To see how to purchase assets on account, complete the following steps.

Date   *Description of Transaction*

11/21   Purchased notebook computer equipment on account from The Business Store, Invoice BOS44, for a total of $400, terms Net 30 days.

1.   Record the 11/21/20XX credit purchase using the Enter Bills icon on the Home page. In the Vendor name field, select The Business Store, Memo: Invoice No. BOS 44.

2.   Click on Expenses tab and complete the following fields:

      Account: 14000, Computer Equipment
      Amount: 400.00
      Memo: Notebook computer

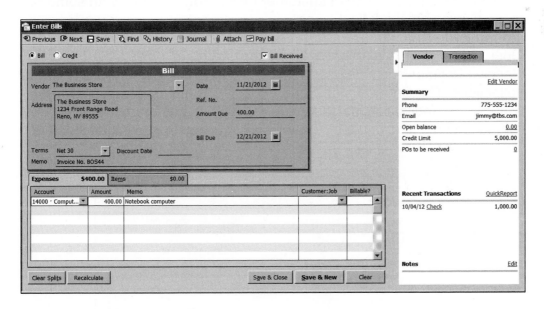

3. When satisfied, click Save & Close.

4. Backup your work. (*HINT:* Menu Bar; File, Save Copy or Backup) Name backup file **Your Name Chapter 4 Vendors.**

5. Exit QuickBooks or continue on to the next section.

CUSTOMERS

Now that you have purchased items from vendors, you are ready to sell that inventory. To do that, you need to learn how to use QuickBooks' customers and receivables tasks. This section shows you how to establish customer records and defaults and explains how QuickBooks' customer work flow system is organized. *Accounts receivable* is a group of accounts that show the amounts customers owe for services or products sold on credit. Credit transactions from customers are called *accounts receivable transactions*.

Customer receipts work similarly to paying vendor invoices. A *customer invoice* is defined as a request for payment to a customer for products or services sold.

The Customer pane on your Home page is where you perform all the tasks related to customers and receivables. QuickBooks' Customers pane shows the work flow of customer tasks. You will work with some of these Customers work flow icons.

Once a new invoice is recorded using the Create Invoices icon, the Receive Payments icon is used to record customer payments or collections. The Create Sales Receipts icon is used for cash sales. The Refunds & Credits icon is used when dissatisfied customers receive a refund or some kind of consideration resulting from a previous sale.

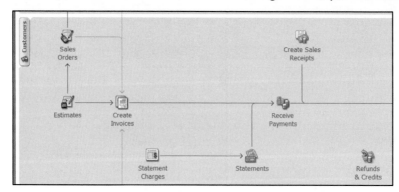

QuickBooks also provides a Customer Center (Navigation Bar; 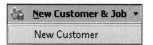) to track tasks related to customers and receivables. The center provides easy access to customer records, contact information, transaction details, and history. The Customer Center is the starting point for managing customers and the tracking of items sold.

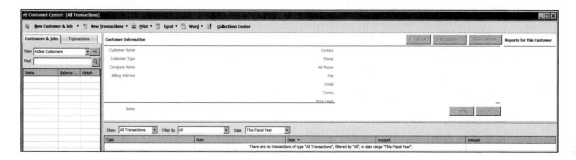

Customer Records

On the Customer Center Home page, you set up customers and receivables.

Follow these steps to set up customer records and defaults.

1. On the Navigation Pane, select Customers.

2. In the Tasks area, use the New Customer & Job pulldown menu to select New Customer.

3. If the New Feature window appears, read it then click OK. The New Customer window appears.

4. Complete the Address Info fields shown here.

Customer Name:	**Audio Answers**
Opening Balance:	**0.00** as of **10/01/20XX (current year)**
Company Name:	**Audio Answers**
First Name:	**Cathleen**
Last Name:	**McClure**
Contact:	Cathleen McClure (completed automatically)
Phone:	**303-555-9312**

FAX: **303-555-1234**
E-mail: **cathleen@audio.biz**
Addresses: **113 Aspen Drive**
                      Telluride, CO 80010

Click [Copy >>]. The Add Shipping Address Information window
appears. Check the information, then click [**OK**].

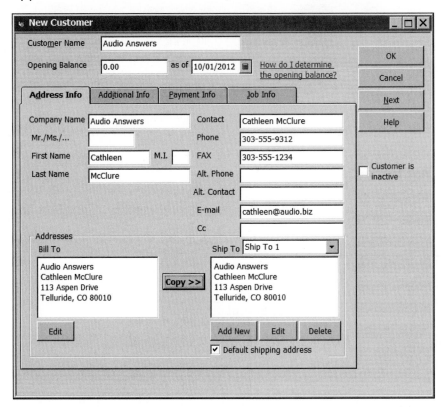

Additional Info tab:

Type: Retail
Terms: Net 30
Preferred Send Method: Mail

Payment Info tab:

Account No. **AA1**
Credit limit: **7,500.00**
Pref. Pay. Method: Check

5.   Check the information recorded. Click [Next].

6.   Enter the following customers:

Customer Name:	**iPrint Design**
Opening Balance:	**0.00** as of **10/01/20XX (current year)**
Company Name:	**iPrint Design**
First Name:	**Rolo**
Last Name:	**Kalm**
Contact:	Rolo Kalm
Phone:	**310-555-2367**
FAX:	**310-555-2368**
E-mail:	**rolo@iprint.com**
Addresses:	**4900 Springer Drive**
	Palos Verdes, CA 90212
Type:	Retail
Terms:	Net 30
Preferred Send Method:	Mail
Account No.:	**IP2**
Credit limit:	**7,500.00**
Preferred Payment Method:	Check

Customer Name:	**Video Solutions**
Opening Balance:	**0.00** as of **10/01/20XX (current year)**
Company Name:	**Video Solutions**
First Name:	**Lyman**
Last Name:	**Hudson**
Contact:	Lyman Hudson
Phone:	**727-555-0613**
FAX:	**727-555-0615**
E-mail:	**lh@video.com**

Addresses:	**86113 Ginnie Blvd.**
	Fanning Springs, FL 34688
Type:	Retail
Terms:	Net 30
Preferred Send Method:	Mail
Account No.:	**VS3**
Credit limit:	**7,500.00**
Preferred Payment Method:	Check

7. Click [OK] to return to Customer desktop.

Customer List

The **customer** list shows information about the customers with whom you do business. Follow these steps to display the customer list.

1. If necessary, go to the Customer Center; click on Customer & Jobs tab in the left pane. The Customer List appears. Observe you can view list by All Customers, Active Customers, Customers with Open Balances, Customers with Overdue Invoices, Customers with Almost Due Invoices, or Custom Filter.

2. Click on the [→] button at the top of the Customer list to show the full list only.

3. Click on the [←] button at the top right of the Customer list to show list and details.

4. To see the detailed record and transaction history of a specific customer, double click on the customer name in the customer list. Information about the customer will appear in the right pane of the Customer Center.

Customers & Accounts Receivables and Sales Reports

QuickBooks' Report Center provides many customer, receivable, and sales reports that you will use in this chapter. Customers & Receivables reports provide information about A/R Aging, Customer Balance, Lists, and other related reports.

Customers & Receivables - A/R Aging (what my customers owe me and what is overdue). A partial window is shown below. Scroll down the Customers & Receivables report center to see more.

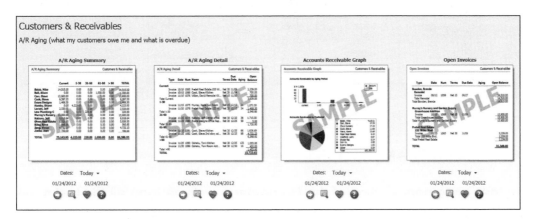

Lists

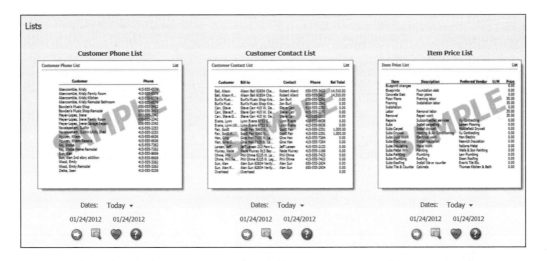

Sales reports include many Sales by Customer, Sales by Item, and Sales by Rep types of reports. In the Report Center, select Sales. A partial list of reports is shown on the next page. Scroll down the Sales Report Center to see more.

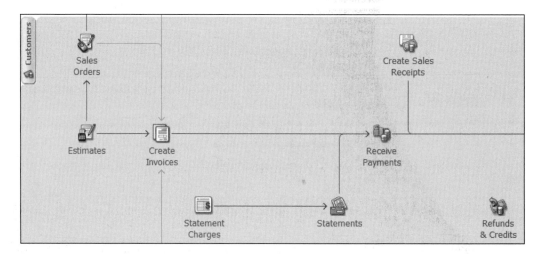

CUSTOMER TRANSACTIONS

In the Customers section of the Home page, you perform all the tasks related to customers and accounts receivables. In this section, you work with some of these features.

In QuickBooks, all information about a sale on account is recorded on the Create Invoice form. Then, QuickBooks takes the necessary information from the Invoice window and automatically creates the transaction's debits and credits. Credit sales from customers are posted to both the General Ledger and to the customers and receivables accounts. In accounting, customers and receivables accounts grouped together are called the *accounts receivable ledger*.

You use QuickBooks' Create Invoices icon to record credit sales to customers. *Credit sales* or sales on account refer to sales made to customers that will be paid for later. Your Name Retailers offers customers payment terms of Net 30 days.

Sales Invoices

The transaction you are going to record is:

Date   *Description of Transaction*

11/15/20XX   Sold 5 eBooks (PDF files) on account to iPrint Design for a total credit sale of $250, Sales No. 1.

Follow these steps to enter the transaction.

1.   On your Home page, click on the Create Invoices icon.

2.   The Create Invoices window appears.

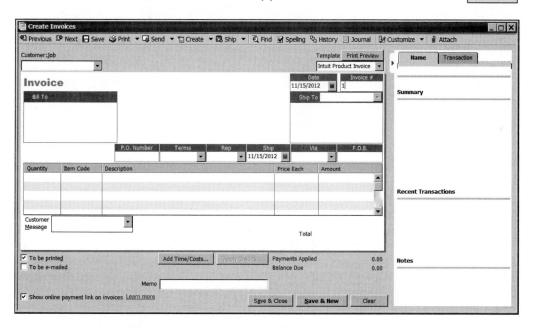

3.   Complete the fields shown here.

Customer: iPrint Design
Date: **11/15/20XX**
Invoice #:   1 is completed automatically
Qty.:   **5**

Item Code:	eBook
Description:	PDF files is completed automatically
Unit Price:	50.00 is completed automatically
Amount:	250.00 is completed automatically

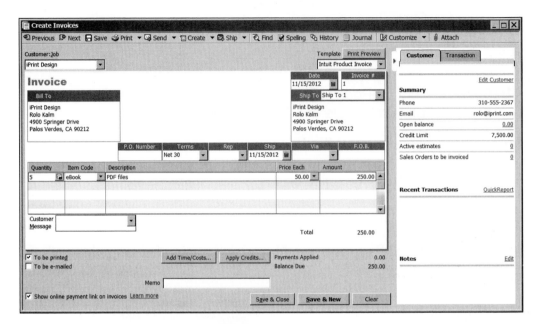

4. When satisfied, click **Save & New**.

5. If Check Spelling on Form window appears, select **Ignore All**.

6. Record the following credit sales.

Date	Description of Transaction
11/15/20XX	Sold 15 Podcasts (audio files) on account to Audio Answers for a total credit sale of $450, Sales No. 2.
11/15/20XX	Sold 8 TV Programs (video files) on account to Video Solutions for a total credit sale of $480, Sales No. 3.

7. Click **Save & Close**.

8. Look at how QuickBooks journalizes these sales by displaying the 11/15/20XX Journal. (Report Center; Accountant & Taxes, Journal, date is 11/15/20XX)

Your Name Retailers Inc.
Journal
November 15, 2012

Trans #	Type	Date	Num	Adj	Name	Memo	Account	Debit	Credit
21	Invoice	11/15/2012	1		iPrint Design		11000 · Accounts Receivable	250.00	
					iPrint Design	PDF files	46000 · Sales		250.00
					iPrint Design	PDF files	12100 · Inventory Asset		125.00
					iPrint Design	PDF files	50001 · *Cost of Goods Sold	125.00	
								375.00	375.00
22	Invoice	11/15/2012	2		Audio Answers		11000 · Accounts Receivable	450.00	
					Audio Answers	audio files	46000 · Sales		450.00
					Audio Answers	audio files	12100 · Inventory Asset		225.00
					Audio Answers	audio files	50001 · *Cost of Goods Sold	225.00	
								675.00	675.00
23	Invoice	11/15/2012	3		Video Solutions		11000 · Accounts Receivable	480.00	
					Video Solutions	video files	46000 · Sales		480.00
					Video Solutions	video files	12100 · Inventory Asset		240.00
					Video Solutions	video files	50001 · *Cost of Goods Sold	240.00	
								720.00	720.00
TOTAL								**1,770.00**	**1,770.00**

9. Look closely at the accounts debited and credited for the sale made to In Print Design.

    Observe that *both* the sales price, $250, and the cost of the inventory item are debited and credited. When Your Name Retailers sells PDF files the customer pays $50 each (5 PDF files were sold for a total of $250). When Your Name Retailers buys PDF files from the vendor, it pays $25 x 5 = $125. QuickBooks tracks both the sales price *and* the purchase price when items are sold. The sales price is debited and credited to AR/customer and Sales; the cost of the item is debited and credited to Cost of Goods Sold and Inventory, respectively. This entry keeps the Inventory account perpetually up to date.

10. Close the Journal without saving.

Inventory

Before recording more sales, let's look at the status of inventory on November 15, 20XX (use your current year). Follow these steps to do that.

1. From Menu Bar select Lists; Item List. The Item List appears.

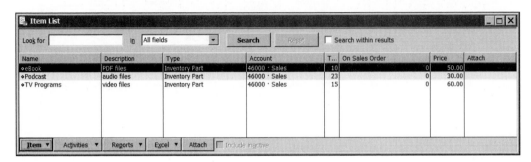

Observe that the following quantities are on hand as of 11/15/20XX:

eBook	PDF files	10
Podcast	audio files	23
TV Programs	video files	15

2. Close the Item List.

Sales Returns

When a customer returns a product or requires a refund, you can create a customer credit memo with the Credit Memo/Refunds form.

The following transaction is for a sales return.

Date	*Description of Transaction*
11/17/20XX	Audio Answers returned 2 Podcasts (audio files).

Follow these steps to enter the sales return.

1. On the Home page in the Customers pane, click on the Refunds & Credits icon.

Refunds & Credits

2.   Select Audio Answers as the Customer.

3.   Type **11/17/20XX** in the date field.

4.   In the Item field, select Podcast.

5.   Type **2** in the Qty. field.

6.   Compare your Create Credit Memo/Refunds window to the one shown here.

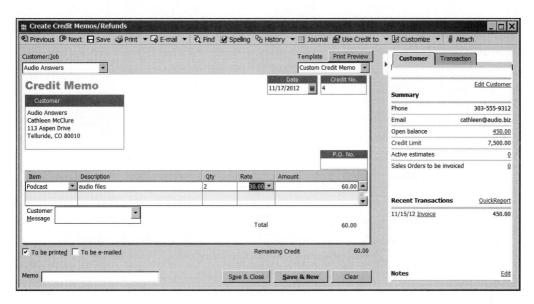

7.   When satisfied, click [Save & Close].

8.   When the Available Credit window appears, select Apply to an Invoice radio button. Then click [OK].

9.   When Apply Credits to Invoices window appears, confirm the Audio Answers 11/15/20XX Invoice is checked.

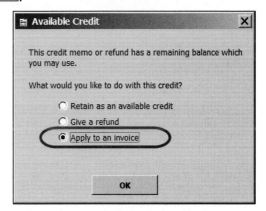

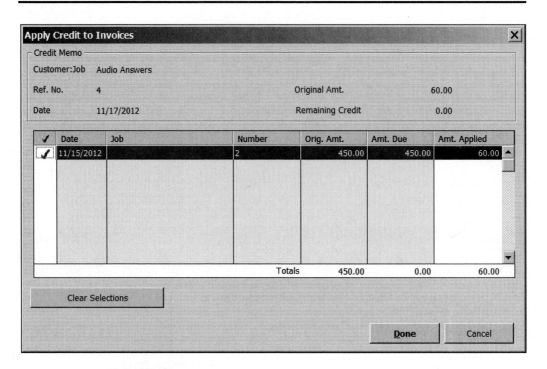

10. Click 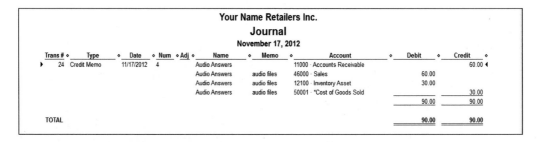 to apply the credit to the invoice.

11. Let's see how this entry is journalized. Display the 11/17/20XX Journal. (Report Center; Accountant & Taxes, Journal, date is 11/17/20XX) Close Journal without saving it.

Your Name Retailers Inc.
Journal
November 17, 2012

Trans #	Type	Date	Num	Adj	Name	Memo	Account	Debit	Credit
24	Credit Memo	11/17/2012	4		Audio Answers		11000 · Accounts Receivable		60.00
					Audio Answers	audio files	46000 · Sales	60.00	
					Audio Answers	audio files	12100 · Inventory Asset	30.00	
					Audio Answers	audio files	50001 · *Cost of Goods Sold		30.00
								90.00	90.00
TOTAL								90.00	90.00

12. Display the Customer Balance Detail Report to see how the accounts receivable account records customer transactions. (*Hint:* Report Center, Customers & Receivables, Customer Balance, Customer Balance Detail, All Dates) Observe that the balance in the Audio Answers account is reduced by the amount of the 11/17/20XX return. Also, notice that the Total on the report is $1,120. This total should agree with the 11/17 balance for Account No. 11000, Accounts Receivable.

Your Name Retailers Inc.
Customer Balance Detail
All Transactions

Type	Date	Num	Account	Amount	Balance
Audio Answers					
Invoice	11/15/2012	2	11000 · Accounts Receivable	450.00	450.00 ◀
Credit Memo	11/17/2012	4	11000 · Accounts Receivable	-60.00	390.00
Total Audio Answers				390.00	390.00
iPrint Design					
Invoice	11/15/2012	1	11000 · Accounts Receivable	250.00	250.00
Total iPrint Design				250.00	250.00
Video Solutions					
Invoice	11/15/2012	3	11000 · Accounts Receivable	480.00	480.00
Total Video Solutions				480.00	480.00
TOTAL				**1,120.00**	**1,120.00**

✓ 13.   Close the Customer Balance Detail report without saving.

✓ 14.   Display the Balance Sheet Detail Report From 10/01/20XX To
11/20/20XX. (*Hint:* Report Center, Company & Financial, Balance
Sheet & Net Worth, Balance Sheet Detail.) Notice the Account No.
11000, Accounts Receivable, shows the same balance as the
Customer Balance Detail, $1,120.00.

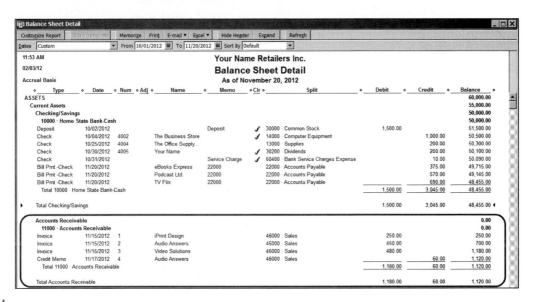

✓ 15.   Close the report without saving and close the report center.

Credit Card Sales

Your Name Retailers accepts credit cards for customer sales but does not use QuickBooks credit card processing service. (QuickBooks charges a fee for processing credit card sales.) Observe that on the Navigation Bar, there is a Cards & eChecks icon [Cards & eChecks]. Also, within the Home Page's Do More with QuickBooks area, there is a link to Accept credit cards - low rates. This takes you to QuickBooks' credit card processing service. Do *not* use the Credit Card link, it will cost you.

Your Name Retailers Inc. is set up to accept credit cards for customer payments and processes credit card sales themselves at their bank, Home State Bank. For our purposes, you will see how a company can process credit cards but you will *not* set up the online credit card processing.

The transaction you are going to record is:

Date   *Description of Transaction*

11/18   Sold 5 eBooks for $250; 8 Podcasts for $240; and 6 TV Programs for $360; for total credit card sales of $850, Sales No. 1.

Follow these steps to enter a new customer on the fly and record credit card sales.

1. From the Customers pane on the Home page, select Create Sales Receipts. The Enter Sales Receipts window appears.

2. Type **11/18/20XX** in the Date field.

3. Accept the default Sales No.

4. In the Customer Name field, select <Add New>. On the New Customer form, complete these fields.

> Customer Name: **Credit Card Sales**
> Opening Balance   **0.00** as of **10/01/20XX**

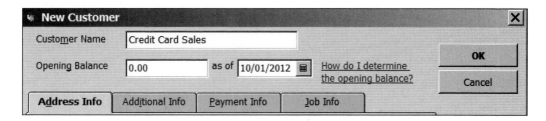

Payment Info tab:

Account No.:   **CCS**
Preferred Payment Method:
Select <Add New>. In the
Payment Method field, type
Credit Card. In the Payment
Type field, select Cash. Click
<OK>.

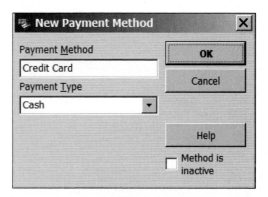

The New Customer window
looks like this:

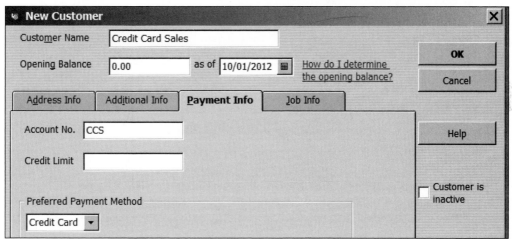

5.   Click [OK]. You are returned to the Enter Sales Receipts
     form. Credit Cards Sales is shown in the Customer:Job. Observe
     that the Sales No. field is completed automatically with the number
     1, and that the Payment Method field shows Credit Card.

6.   In the Item field, select eBook.

7.   Type **5** in the Qty. field.

8.   Go to the Item field, select Podcast.

9.   Type **8** in the Qty. field.

10.   Go to the Item field, select TV Programs.

11.   Type **6** in the Qty. field.

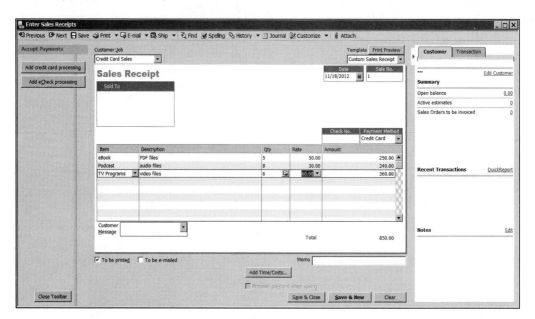

12.   Click [S̲ave & Close]. Ignore the spelling window about PDF.

13.   To see how this transaction is journalized, display the Journal for 11/18/20XX. Observe that each item amount is individually debited and credited to Undeposited Funds, Sales, Costs of Goods Sold, and Inventory.

Your Name Retailers Inc.
Journal
November 18, 2012

Trans #	Type	Date	Num	Adj	Name	Memo	Account	Debit	Credit
25	Sales Receipt	11/18/2012	1		Credit Card Sales		12000 · Undeposited Funds	850.00	
					Credit Card Sales	-MULTIPLE-	46000 · Sales		850.00 ◀
					Credit Card Sales	-MULTIPLE-	12100 · Inventory Asset		425.00
					Credit Card Sales	-MULTIPLE-	50001 · *Cost of Goods Sold	425.00	
								1,275.00	1,275.00
	TOTAL							1,275.00	1,275.00

The Memo column shows MULTIPLE. This indicates more than one inventory item. Drill down (double-click) MULTIPLE to see the Enter Sales Receipts window which indicates the three items sold: eBooks (5 PDF files), Podcast (8 audio files), and TV Programs (6 video files). Close the Enter Sales Receipts window and the Journal.

Customer Payments

When a customer sends you a payment, enter the customer payment on the Receive Payment form. You can then apply the payment to the invoices that are due. A payment might cover one or more invoices, or it may not completely cover an invoice. You can select which invoice to settle against a payment as well as the amount to apply to each invoice. *Or,* you can have QuickBooks automatically apply the payment to invoices in chronological order from the oldest outstanding invoice.

In the following transactions, customers pay their outstanding invoices.

Date   *Description of Transaction*

11/23   Received a check in full payment of Audio Answers'
               account, $390.

Using the payment from Audio Answers as an example, follow these steps to record a customer payment.

1. From the Customers pane on the Home page, select
    Receive Payments icon.

2. Complete the following fields on the Receive Payments form:

    Received From: Audio Answers
    Date: **11/23/20XX**

Amount:	**390.00**
Payment method:	Check is automatically completed
Customer balance:	$390.00 is automatically completed

3. A check mark is placed next to the 11/15 invoice automatically. Notice the original amount $450.00 was reduced to $390.00 by the previously applied credit memo for $60.00 since Audio Answers returned merchandise.

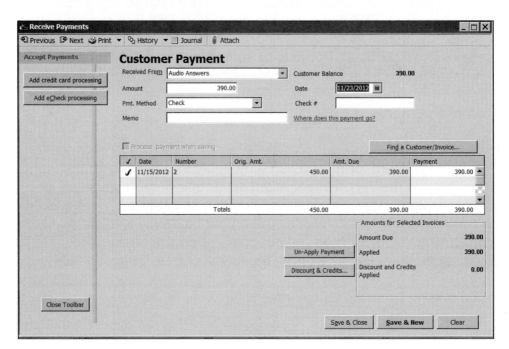

4. Click 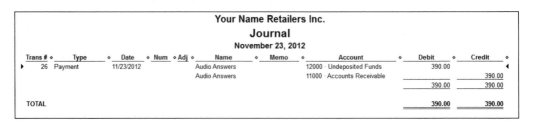 .

5. Display the 11/23/20XX Journal. When a customer payment is received, Undeposited Funds and Accounts Receivable are debited and credited respectively. (The example shows the customer payment received from Audio Answers.)

Your Name Retailers Inc.
Journal
November 23, 2012

Trans #	Type	Date	Num	Adj	Name	Memo	Account	Debit	Credit
26	Payment	11/23/2012			Audio Answers		12000 · Undeposited Funds	390.00	
					Audio Answers		11000 · Accounts Receivable		390.00
								390.00	390.00
TOTAL								**390.00**	**390.00**

What are undeposited funds? Account No. 12000, Undeposited Funds, is a cash account for amounts received from customers but not yet deposited to the bank account. When bank deposits are made, Undeposited Funds will be credited and Home State Bank-Cash will be debited. You can think of undeposited funds as a clearing account. The undeposited funds account holds the cash until they are deposited and cleared by the bank. The November bank statement will show which customer payments cleared Account No. 10000, Home State Bank-Cash, which is Your Name Retailers' bank account.

6. Record the two November 24, 20XX payments received from customers.

Date	Description of Transaction

11/24   Received a check in full payment of iPrint Design's account, $250.

11/24   Received a check in full payment of Video Solutions' account, $480.

7. Click ⬚ Save & Close ⬚ to return to Home page.

8. After you record the customer checks received on 11/24 and physically deposited the 11/23 and 11/24 checks received into the Home State Bank, you make the bank deposit entry. On the Banking pane of the Home page, click on the Record Deposits icon.

9. The Payments to Deposit window appears.

10. Place a check mark next to the 11/23 and 11/24 checks included in the deposit. (Customer checks for $390.00 +$250.00 +$480.00 were deposited.) Place a check mark next to Credit Card Sales $850.00. Compare your Payments to Deposit window to the one shown on the next page.

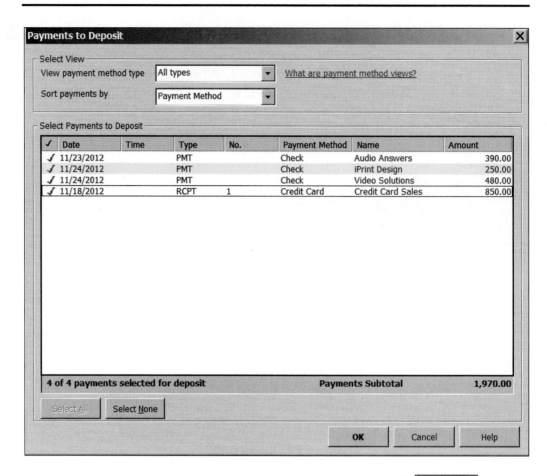

11. The Total amount of the deposit is $1,970.00. Click [OK].

12. The Make Deposits window appears. Observe that the Deposit To field shows Home State Bank-Cash. Compare your Make Deposits window to the one shown on the next page.

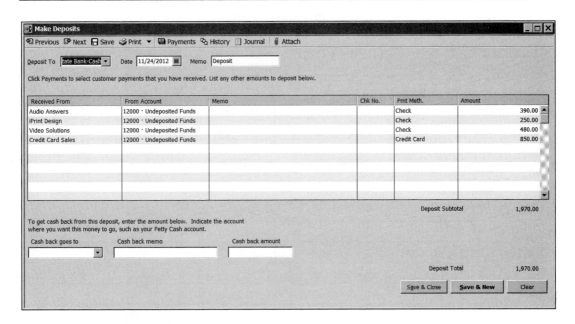

13.   Click   Save & Close   . You are returned to the Home page.

14.   Backup your work. The suggested file name is **Your Name Chapter 4 November.QBB**. Exit QuickBooks or continue to the next section.

> **Comment:**
> Separation of duties means work is divided between different employees to insure data integrity and minimize the opportunity for wrongdoing. This is a basic internal control. For example to keep employees from stealing customer payments, the tasks: opening the mail, recording customer payments, and making deposits at the bank are assigned to three different employees.

ACCOUNT RECONCILIATION

1.   To reconcile Account No. 10000 for November, use the bank statement shown on the next page. (*HINT:* See previous chapter for October's Account Reconciliation steps.)

Statement of Account			Your Name Retailers	
Home State Bank			Your address	
November 1 to November 30		Account # 89123631	Reno, NV	
REGULAR CHECKING				
Previous Balance	10/31	**$50,290.00**		
Deposits(+)		1,970.00		
Checks (-)		1,835.00		
Service Charges (-)	11/30	10.00		
Ending Balance	11/30	**50,415.00**		
DEPOSITS				
	11/24	1,120.00	Customers	
	11/24	850.00	Credit Card	
CHECKS (Asterisk * indicates break in check number sequence)				
	11/3	200.00	4004	
	11/25	375.00	4006*	
	11/25	570.00	4007	
	11/25	690.00	4008	

2.   After placing check marks beside the cleared deposits and checks per the bank statement, compare your window to the following.

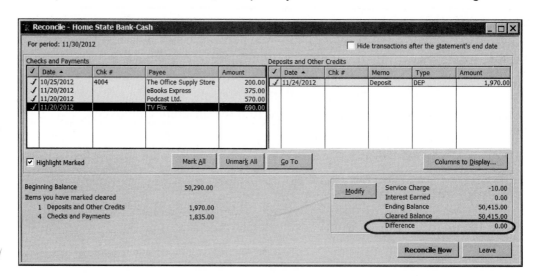

3.   The Reconcile - Home State Bank-Cash shows a Difference of $00.00.

4.   Click [Reconcile Now], Wait, then select Display Detail.

Your Name Retailers Inc.
Reconciliation Detail
10000 · Home State Bank-Cash, Period Ending 11/30/2012

Type	◇	Date	◇ Num	◇	Name	◇ Clr ◇	Amount	◇	Balance	◇
Beginning Balance									50,290.00	
Cleared Transactions										
Checks and Payments - 5 items										
▶ Check		10/25/2012	4004		The Office Supply...	✓	-200.00		-200.00	◀
Bill Pmt -Check		11/20/2012			TV Flix	✓	-690.00		-890.00	
Bill Pmt -Check		11/20/2012			Podcast Ltd.	✓	-570.00		-1,460.00	
Bill Pmt -Check		11/20/2012			eBooks Express	✓	-375.00		-1,835.00	
Check		11/30/2012				✓	-10.00		-1,845.00	
Total Checks and Payments							-1,845.00		-1,845.00	
Deposits and Credits - 1 item										
Deposit		11/24/2012				✓	1,970.00		1,970.00	
Total Deposits and Credits							1,970.00		1,970.00	
Total Cleared Transactions							125.00		125.00	
Cleared Balance							125.00		50,415.00	
Register Balance as of 11/30/2012							125.00		50,415.00	
Ending Balance							125.00		50,415.00	

---

5.   Close the Reconciliation Detail window.

REPORTS

Print the following reports. Compare your reports to the ones shown on the next pages. If you have made errors in your entries, void and edit your original entries to correct your reports. (*HINT:* See pages 84-86.)

1.   Trial Balance from 10/01/20XX to 11/30/20XX.

Your Name Retailers Inc.
Trial Balance
As of November 30, 2012

	Nov 30, 12	
	Debit	Credit
10000 · Home State Bank-Cash	▶ 50,415.00 ◀	
11000 · Accounts Receivable	0.00	
12000 · Undeposited Funds	0.00	
12100 · Inventory Asset	650.00	
13000 · Supplies	2,700.00	
18000 · Prepaid Insurance	2,500.00	
14000 · Computer Equipment	2,400.00	
15000 · Furniture and Equipment	4,000.00	
22000 · Accounts Payable		400.00
26000 · Your Name Notes Payable		20,000.00
30000 · Common Stock		41,500.00
30200 · Dividends	200.00	
46000 · Sales		1,970.00
50001 · *Cost of Goods Sold	985.00	
60400 · Bank Service Charges Expense	20.00	
TOTAL	63,870.00	63,870.00

2. Journal 11/01/20XX to 11/30/20XX.

Your Name Retailers Inc.
Journal
November 2012

Trans #	Type	Date	Num	Adj	Name	Memo	Account	Debit	Credit
12	Bill	11/02/2012			Podcast Ltd.	Invoice No. 5	22000 · Accounts Payable		300.00 ◄
					Podcast Ltd.	audio files	12100 · Inventory Asset	300.00	
								300.00	300.00
13	Bill	11/03/2012			eBooks Express	Invoice 90eB	22000 · Accounts Payable		375.00
					eBooks Express	PDF files	12100 · Inventory Asset	375.00	
								375.00	375.00
14	Bill	11/03/2012			TV Flix	Invoice No. 210TV	22000 · Accounts Payable		750.00
					TV Flix	video files	12100 · Inventory Asset	750.00	
								750.00	750.00
15	Bill	11/05/2012			Podcast Ltd.	Invoice No. 78PS	22000 · Accounts Payable		270.00
					Podcast Ltd.	audio files	12100 · Inventory Asset	270.00	
								270.00	270.00
16	Credit	11/10/2012	CM1		TV Flix	Invoice No. 210TV	22000 · Accounts Payable	60.00	
					TV Flix	video files	12100 · Inventory Asset		60.00
								60.00	60.00
17	Bill Pmt -Check	11/20/2012			eBooks Express	22000	10000 · Home State Bank-Cash		375.00
					eBooks Express	22000	22000 · Accounts Payable	375.00	
								375.00	375.00
18	Bill Pmt -Check	11/20/2012			Podcast Ltd.	22000	10000 · Home State Bank-Cash		570.00
					Podcast Ltd.	22000	22000 · Accounts Payable	570.00	
								570.00	570.00
19	Bill Pmt -Check	11/20/2012			TV Flix	22000	10000 · Home State Bank-Cash		690.00
					TV Flix	22000	22000 · Accounts Payable	690.00	
								690.00	690.00
20	Bill	11/21/2012			The Business Store	Invoice No. BOS44	22000 · Accounts Payable		400.00
					The Business Store	Notebook computer	14000 · Computer Equipment	400.00	
								400.00	400.00
21	Invoice	11/15/2012	1		iPrint Design		11000 · Accounts Receivable	250.00	
					iPrint Design	PDF files	46000 · Sales		250.00
					iPrint Design	PDF files	12100 · Inventory Asset		125.00
					iPrint Design	PDF files	50001 · *Cost of Goods Sold	125.00	
								375.00	375.00
22	Invoice	11/15/2012	2		Audio Answers		11000 · Accounts Receivable	450.00	
					Audio Answers	audio files	46000 · Sales		450.00
					Audio Answers	audio files	12100 · Inventory Asset		225.00
					Audio Answers	audio files	50001 · *Cost of Goods Sold	225.00	
								675.00	675.00
23	Invoice	11/15/2012	3		Video Solutions		11000 · Accounts Receivable	480.00	
					Video Solutions	video files	46000 · Sales		480.00
					Video Solutions	video files	12100 · Inventory Asset		240.00
					Video Solutions	video files	50001 · *Cost of Goods Sold	240.00	
								720.00	720.00
24	Credit Memo	11/17/2012	4		Audio Answers		11000 · Accounts Receivable		60.00
					Audio Answers	audio files	46000 · Sales	60.00	
					Audio Answers	audio files	12100 · Inventory Asset	30.00	
					Audio Answers	audio files	50001 · *Cost of Goods Sold		30.00
								90.00	90.00

Continued on the next page

25	Sales Receipt	11/18/2012	1	Credit Card Sales		12000 · Undeposited Funds	850.00	
				Credit Card Sales	-MULTIPLE-	46000 · Sales		850.00
				Credit Card Sales	-MULTIPLE-	12100 · Inventory Asset		425.00
				Credit Card Sales	-MULTIPLE-	50001 · *Cost of Goods Sold	425.00	
							1,275.00	1,275.00
26	Payment	11/23/2012		Audio Answers		12000 · Undeposited Funds	390.00	
				Audio Answers		11000 · Accounts Receivable		390.00
							390.00	390.00
27	Payment	11/24/2012		iPrint Design		12000 · Undeposited Funds	250.00	
				iPrint Design		11000 · Accounts Receivable		250.00
							250.00	250.00
28	Payment	11/24/2012		Video Solutions		12000 · Undeposited Funds	480.00	
				Video Solutions		11000 · Accounts Receivable		480.00
							480.00	480.00
29	Deposit	11/24/2012			Deposit	10000 · Home State Bank-Cash	1,970.00	
				-MULTIPLE-	Deposit	12000 · Undeposited Funds		1,970.00
							1,970.00	1,970.00
30	Check	11/30/2012			Service Charge	10000 · Home State Bank-Cash		10.00
					Service Charge	60400 · Bank Service Charges Ex...	10.00	
							10.00	10.00
TOTAL							10,025.00	10,025.00

3. Item List.

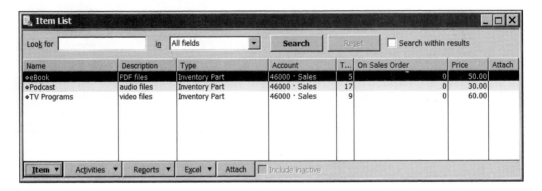

4.   Transaction List by Vendor 11/01/20XX to 11/30/20XX.

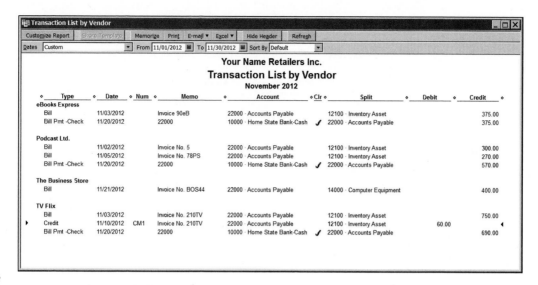

5.   Purchase by Item Summary 11/01/20XX to 11/30/20XX. (*Hint:* This is a Purchases report.)

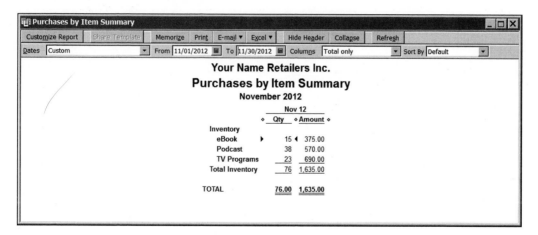

6.   Purchases by Vendor Detail 11/01/20XX to 11/30/20XX.

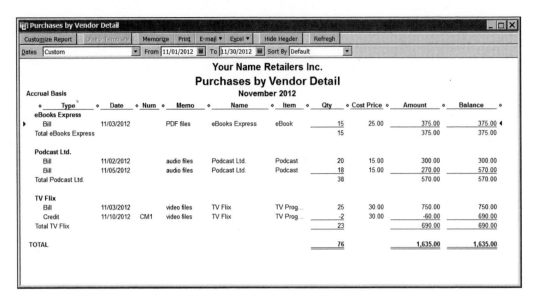

7.   Customer Contact List.

8.   Transaction List by Customer 11/01/20XX to 11/30/20XX.

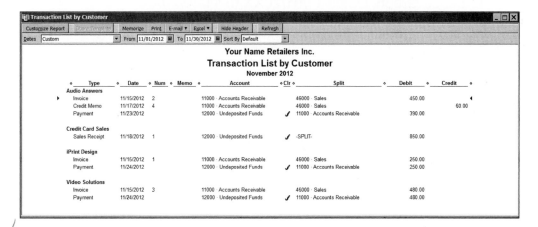

9.   Income by Customer Summary 11/01/20XX to 11/30/20XX. (*Hint:* Company & Financial reports.)

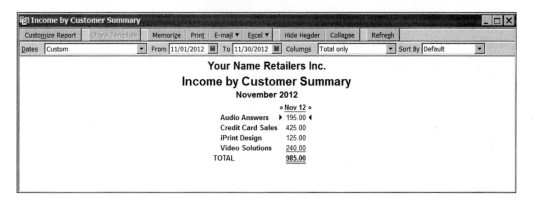

10. Income and Expense Graph: *Hint:* Company & Financial, Income & Expense Graph, Dates 11/01/20XX to 11/30/20XX.

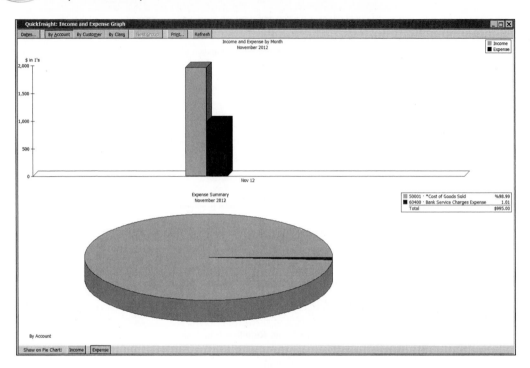

11. Sales by Item Summary 11/01/20XX to 11/30/20XX. (*Hint:* Sales report.)

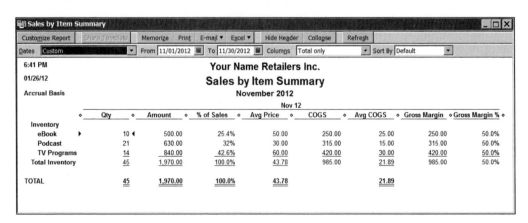

SERVICES

QuickBooks includes many add-on fees for online services and apps.

1. From the Menu Bar, select Online Services. Observe that QuickBooks offers many online services. Since Your Name Retailers Inc. does not have employees, sell online, or track time and is already incorporated; additional QuickBooks solutions are limited. Any of these services can be built into QuickBooks if a company elects to pay and use them. Browse the additional services offered to see them in action or learn more.

2. From the Navigation Bar if you select 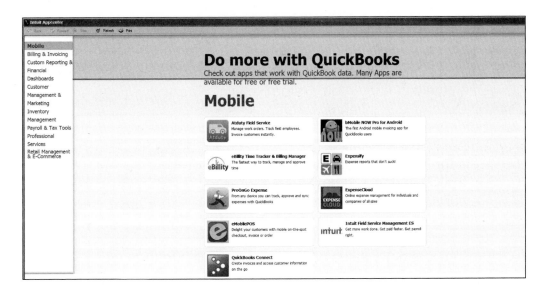 , the following screen appears if you are online. Browse the additional services offered to see them in action or learn more.

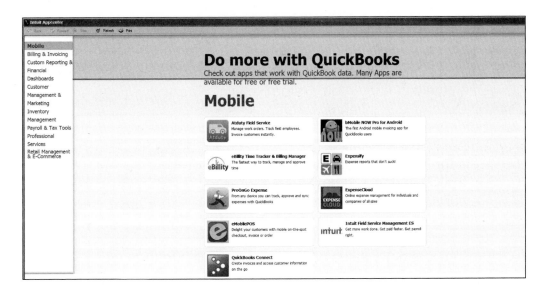

3. When through, close the Intuit Appcenter window. If necessary, close all windows.

BACKUP CHAPTER 4 DATA

1. Backup your work to your USB drive. (*HINT:* File; Save Copy or Backup) Name your file **Your Name Chapter 4 End**.

2. Transfer backup to your USB drive.

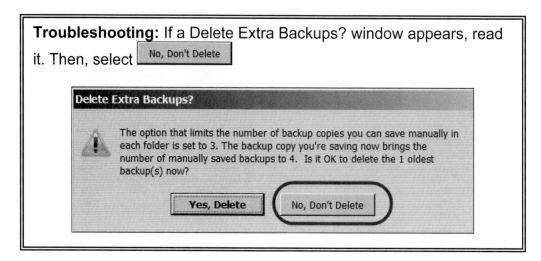

3. Exit QuickBooks or continue with the next section.

SUMMARY AND REVIEW

OBJECTIVES:

1. Open the company, Your Name Retailers Inc.
2. Enter items and inventory preferences.
3. Enter vendor records.
4. Enter inventory items.
5. Print the vendor list and item list.
6. Enter bills and record purchase returns.
7. Pay bills.
8. Add a vendor and non-inventory item on the fly.
9. Enter customer records and defaults.
10. Record customer sales on account and sales returns.
11. Receive customer payments.
12. Make backups.[2]

---

[2]The chart in the Preface shows you the size of each backup file. Refer to this chart for backing up data. Remember, you can back up to a hard drive location or external media.

RESOURCEFUL QUICKBOOKS

Use QuickBooks Coach to View Tutorials on Vendors, Items, and Customers. Answer the following questions.

1. Vendors: When setting up a new vendor, should you enter an opening balance or enter each unpaid bill? Why?
2. Inventory & Items: How does the video show the setting of preferences for inventory and items? Does this agree with the steps shown in the chapter?
3. Customers: How does the video recommend a customer's name be entered?

Multiple Choice Questions: The Online Learning Center includes the multiple-choice questions at www.mhhe.com/QBessentials2012, select Student Edition, Chapter 4, Multiple Choice.

_____1. A group of posting accounts that shows the amounts owed to vendors or suppliers is called:

  a. Accounts receivable.
  b. Inventory.
  c. Accounts payable.
  d. Entering bills.
  e. All of the above.

_____2. Your Name Retailers describes eBooks as:

  a. Video files.
  b. PDF files.
  c. Audio files.
  d. None of the above.
  e. All of the above.

_____3. QuickBooks Lists include all of the following except:

  a. Items.
  b. Customers.
  c. Vendors.
  d. Accounts.
  e. All are QuickBooks Lists.

_____4.   Products that are purchased for sale are tracked in the
following account:

    a.   Account No. 46000, Sales.
    b.   Account No. 11000, Accounts Receivable.
    c.   Account No. 12100, Inventory.
    d.   Account No. 13000, Supplies.
    e.   None of the above.

_____5.   Which of the following shows information about inventory
items?

    a.   Vendor list.
    b.   Trial Balance.
    c.   Item list.
    d.   Vendor record.
    e.   None of the above.

_____6.   An in-depth view of the amounts the company owes its vendors
as of a selected date.

    a.   Transaction list by vendor.
    b.   Invoice.
    c.   Purchases by item detail.
    d.   A/P aging summary.
    e.   All of the above.

_____7.   When merchandise is returned to the vendor, the following
accounts are debited and credited:

    a.   Dr. Account No. 12100, Inventory; Credit Account No.
50000, Cost of Goods Sold.
    b.   Debit Account No. 50000, Cost of Goods Sold and Account
No. 12100, Inventory; Credit Account No. 5015, Cost of
Goods Sold and Account No. 22000, Accounts Payable.
    c.   Debit Account No. 50000, Cost of Goods Sold and Account
No. 22000, Accounts Payable; Credit Account No. 50000,
Cost of Goods Sold and Account No. 12100, Inventory.
    d.   Debit Account No. 22000 Accounts Payable; credit Account
No. 12100, Inventory.
    e.   None of the above.

_____8.   When a vendor payment is made, the following accounts are debited and credited:

a.   Dr. Account No. 22000, Accounts Payable/vendor; Credit Account No. 10000, Home State Bank-Cash.
b.   Credit Account No. 10000, Home State Bank-Cash; Debit Account No. 12100, Inventory
c.   Debit Account No. 50000, Cost of Goods Sold and Credit Account No. 10000, Home State Bank-Cash.
d.   Debit Account No. 22000 Accounts Payable; credit Account No. 50000, Cost of Goods Sold.
e.   None of the above.

_____9.   The term used for adding a new vendor to a transaction is called:

a.   Drill-down.
b.   A/P.
c.   Inventory item.
d.   On-the-fly.
e.   None of the above.

_____10.   Which report(s) shows the accounts payable balance?

a.   Purchases by vendor detail.
b.   Item list.
c.   Vendor transaction history.
d.   Trial balance.
e.   Both c. and d.

True/Make True: To answer these questions, go online to www.mhhe.com/QBessentials2012, link to Student Edition, Chapter 4, QA Templates. The analysis question at the end of the chapter is also included.

1. Another term for vendor is supplier.

2. A vendor of Your Name Retailers Inc is TV Flix.

3. Credit card sales are recorded using the Home page Pay Bills icon.

4. Purchases from vendors are recorded using Home page Enter Bills icon.

5. Sales to customers are recorded using the Home page Create Invoice icon.

6. Purchases returned to vendors are recorded using the Home page Enter Bills icon.

7. Returns from customers are recorded using the Home page Refunds and Credits icon.

8. Customer payments on account are recorded using Home page Receive Payments icon.

9.   Inventory purchased on account is recorded using the Home page Enter Bills icon.

10. Vendor payments are recorded using Home page Create Cash Receipt icon.

 Exercise 4-1: Follow the instructions below to complete Exercise 4-1.

1. If necessary start QuickBooks and open Your Name Retailers. Restore the Your Name Chapter 4 End file.

2. Identify the Home page icon that will be used to record each of the December transactions listed below.

3.   Record the following transactions during the month of December:

Date	Description of Transaction
√ 12/21	Pay BOS44 to The Business Store for the $400 laptop computer purchase on 11/21.
12/21	Invoice No. 101eB received from eBooks Express for the purchase of 16 PDF files, $25 each, for a total of $400.
12/21	Invoice No. 352TV received from TV Flix for the purchase of 22 video files, $30 each, for a total of $660.
12/21	Invoice No. 95PS received from Podcast Ltd. for the purchase of 12 audio files, $15 each, for a total of $180.
12/23	Returned two PDF files to eBooks Express, CM2 for a total of $50.
12/24	Sold 8 eBooks (PDF files) on account to iPrint Design for a total credit sale of $400, Invoice No. 5.
12/24	Sold 10 Podcasts (audio files) on account to Audio Answers for a total credit sale of $300 Invoice No. 6.
12/24	Sold 12 TV Programs (video files) on account to Video Solutions for a total credit sale of $720, Invoice No. 7.
12/26	Sold 4 eBooks for $200; 8 Podcasts for $240; and 6 TV Programs for $360; for total credit card sales of $800, Sale Receipt No. 2.
12/27	Video Solutions returned 2 TV Programs (video files), $120. Apply to invoice.
12/30	Received a check in full payment of Audio Answers' account, $300.
12/30	Received a check in full payment of iPrint Design's account, $400.

✓12/30   Your Name Retailers pays all outstanding vendor bills for a total of $1,190. (*Hint:* Remember to Set Credit for the 12/23/20XX return to eBooks Express.)

✓12/30   Invoice No. 152PS received from Podcast Ltd. for the purchase of 10 audio files, $15 each, for a total of $150.

✓12/30   Make bank deposit into Home State Bank account, include all undeposited funds, $1,500.

4. Continue with Exercise 4-2.

Exercise 4-2: Follow the instructions below to complete Exercise 4-2. Exercise 4-1 *must* be completed before starting Exercise 4-2.

1. Print the following reports. Your instructor may want these reports saved as PDF files and attached in an email. Refer to the read me box in Chapter 3, page 106, for saving reports as PDFs.

    a. Trial Balance 12/31/20XX.

    b. Journal 12/01/20XX to 12/31/20XX.

    c. Item List.

    d. Transaction List by Vendor 12/01/20XX to 12/31/20XX.

    e. Purchases by Vendor Detail 12/01/20XX to 12/31/20XX.

    f. Transaction List by Customer 12/01/20XX to 12/31/20XX.

    g. Income and Expense Graph: Dates, By Customer, Income 12/01/20XX to 12/31/20XX.

2. If necessary, close all windows. Backup to USB drive. The suggested file name is **Your Name Exercise 4-2 December**.

ANALYSIS QUESTION

Does Your Name Retailers use the periodic or perpetual system for tracking inventory and sales?

Chapter

5

Accounting Cycle and Year End

OBJECTIVES:

1. Restore data from the Exercise 4-2 backup.
2. Record a compound journal entry.
3. Write checks for expenses.
4. Make deposits.
5. Complete account reconciliation.
6. Print a trial balance (unadjusted).
7. Record and post quarterly adjusting entries in the General Journal.
8. Print adjusted trial balance and financial statements.
9. Close the fiscal year.
10. Print a Postclosing Trial Balance.
11. Make backups of Chapter 5 data.[1]

Additional textbook related resources are on the textbook website at www.mhhe.com/QBessentials2012. It includes chapter resources, including online quizzes, etc.

GETTING STARTED:

1. Start QuickBooks. Open Your Name Retailers.

2. If necessary, restore the Your Name Exercise 4-2 December backup file. This backup was made on page 172.

3. To make sure you are starting in the correct place, display the 12/31/20XX (use your current year) trial balance. Compare your trial balance with the one on the next page.

---

[1]The chart in the Preface, page xii, shows the file name and size of each backup file. Refer to this chart for backing up data. Remember, you can back up to a hard drive location or external media.

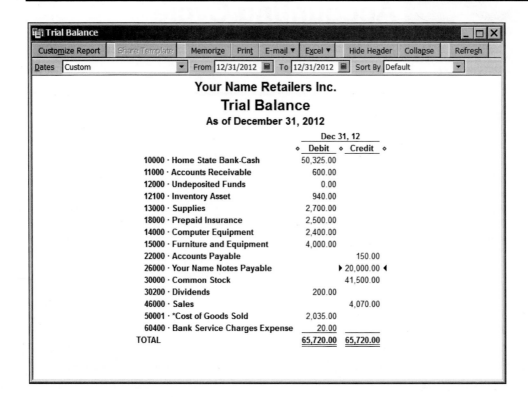

4. Close the trial balance.

COMPOUND TRANSACTIONS

A ***compound transaction*** is an entry that affects three or more accounts. The principle and interest payment on the Your Name Note Payable is an example of a compound transaction. Use QuickBooks' New General Journal Entry window to record compound transactions.

Follow these steps to record a compound journal entry.

1. From the Menu Bar, select Company; Make General Journal Entries.

2. When the Assigning Numbers to Journal Entries screen appears, read it and click OK.

3. The Make General Journal Entries window appears. Uncheck the Adjusting Entry box— ☐ Adjusting Entry .

4. Record the following 12/31/20XX note payable payment. Refer to account distribution below for the appropriate accounts debits and credits.

    Date   *Date of Transaction*

    12/31   Pay $800 to Your Name for note payable principle repayment with interest. The account distribution is:

Acct. No.	Account	Debit	Credit
26000	Your Name Notes Payable	542.00	
63400	Interest Expense	258.00	
10000	Home State Bank-Cash		800.00

5. Compare your Make General Journal Entries window to the one shown here.

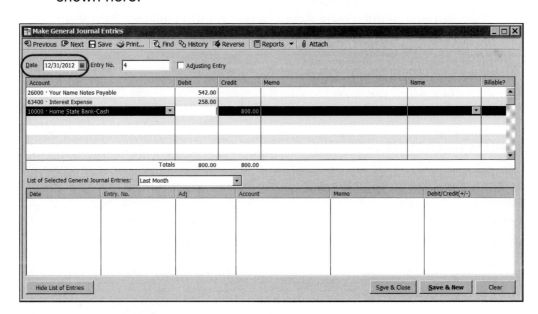

6. Click Save & Close .

WRITE CHECKS

From QuickBooks Home page use the Banking pane's Write Checks icon to issue the following checks:

✓12/31   Issue Check No. 4015 in the amount of $80 for cellular service. (*Hint:* Debit Account No. 68100, Telephone Expense; quick add the vendor, Mobile One.)

✓12/31   Issue Check No. 4016 in the amount of $50 for Internet service. (*Hint:* Debit Account No. 61700, Computer and Internet Expense. Quick add the vendor, ISP.)

✓12/31   Issue Check No. 4017 in the amount of $68 for telephone service. (*Hint:* Debit Account No. 68100, Telephone Expense. Add the vendor, Everywhere Telephone Service.)

✓12/31   Issue Check No. 4018 in the amount of $111 for Electricity/Gas. (*Hint:* Debit Account No. 68600 Utilities. Quick add the vendor, Regional Utilities.)

✓12/31   Issue Check No. 4019 in the amount of $74 for Water/Garbage service. (*Hint:* Debit Account No. 68600 Utilities. Add the vendor, Reno Water/Garbage.)

12/31   Pay $200 Dividend to sole stockholder, Your Name. Check No. 4020 payable to you. Save and close Write Checks window.

CHECK REGISTER

Click on the Check Register icon in the Banking pane of the Home page to see Account No. 10000, Home State Bank-Cash activity. You can enlarge to 10000 Home State Bank-Cash window to see more transactions.

Check Register

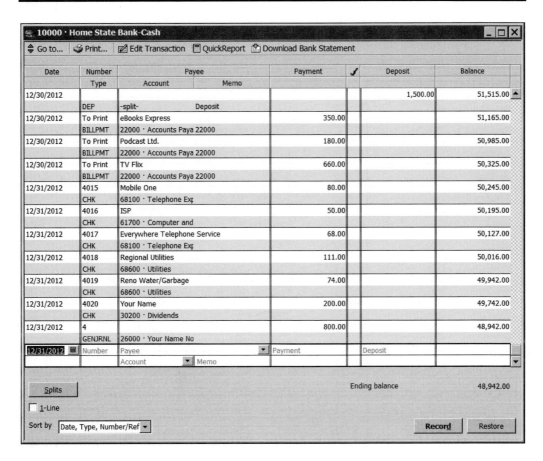

Date	Number	Payee		Payment	✓	Deposit	Balance
	Type	Account	Memo				
12/30/2012						1,500.00	51,515.00
	DEP	-split-	Deposit				
12/30/2012	To Print	eBooks Express		350.00			51,165.00
	BILLPMT	22000 · Accounts Paya 22000					
12/30/2012	To Print	Podcast Ltd.		180.00			50,985.00
	BILLPMT	22000 · Accounts Paya 22000					
12/30/2012	To Print	TV Flix		660.00			50,325.00
	BILLPMT	22000 · Accounts Paya 22000					
12/31/2012	4015	Mobile One		80.00			50,245.00
	CHK	68100 · Telephone Exp					
12/31/2012	4016	ISP		50.00			50,195.00
	CHK	61700 · Computer and					
12/31/2012	4017	Everywhere Telephone Service		68.00			50,127.00
	CHK	68100 · Telephone Exp					
12/31/2012	4018	Regional Utilities		111.00			50,016.00
	CHK	68600 · Utilities					
12/31/2012	4019	Reno Water/Garbage		74.00			49,942.00
	CHK	68600 · Utilities					
12/31/2012	4020	Your Name		200.00			49,742.00
	CHK	30200 · Dividends					
12/31/2012	4			800.00			48,942.00
	GENJRNL	26000 · Your Name No					
12/31/2012	Number	Payee		Payment		Deposit	
		Account	Memo				

Splits

☐ 1-Line

Sort by Date, Type, Number/Ref ▼

Ending balance   48,942.00

Record   Restore

After comparing your Account No. 10000-Home State Bank-Cash account to the register, close.

ACCOUNT RECONCILIATION

You may want to review detailed steps for account reconciliation, pages 88-92. Using the bank statement shown below, reconcile the Home State Bank account. Remember the bank service charge of $10.00.

Follow these steps to complete account reconciliation.

1. From the Banking pane of the Home page, select the Reconcile icon. All checks have cleared the bank. To reconcile, use the bank statement on the next page.

Reconcile

Statement of Account Home State Bank December 1 to December 31, 20XX	Account #0618-3201		Your Name Retailers Your Address Reno, NV	
REGULAR CHECKING				
Previous Balance	11/30	50,415.00		
Deposits		1,500.00		
Checks (-)		2,973.00		
Service Charges (-)	12/31	10.00		
Ending Balance	12/31	**$48,932.00**		
DEPOSITS				
	12/31	300.00	Audio Answers	
	12/31	400.00	iPrint Design	
	12/31	800.00	Credit Card	
CHECKS				
	12/23	400.00		
	12/31	350.00		
	12/31	180.00		
	12/31	660.00		
	12/31	800.00		
	12/31	80.00	4015	
	12/31	50.00	4016	
	12/31	68.00	4017	
	12/31	111.00	4018	
	12/31	74.00	4019	
	12/31	200.00	4020	

2. Reconcile the account. Compare your Reconcile-Home State Bank-Cash screen to the one shown on the next page.

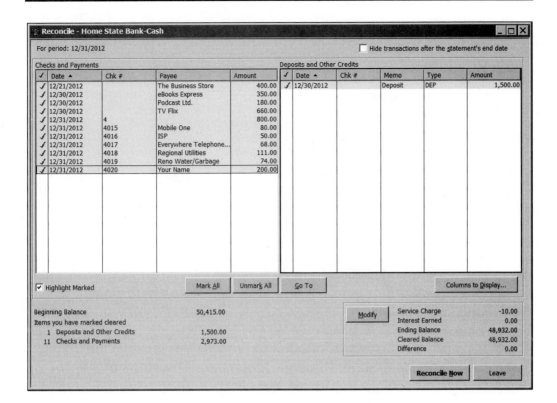

Observe that the Check Register on page 177 shows an ending balance of $48,942.00. The bank statement's ending balance shows $48,932.00. The difference is the bank service charge of $10.00. Once those fees are deducted from the check register balance, the bank statement and check register agree.

3.   Make sure the Difference field shows 0.00. When satisfied, click
     Reconcile Now .

4.   Display the Reconciliation Summary report. When the Reconciliation Report window prompts, This report displays current data, click OK . Compare your Reconciliation Summary report to the one shown on the next page.

Your Name Retailers Inc.
Reconciliation Summary
10000 · Home State Bank-Cash, Period Ending 12/31/2012

	Dec 31, 12
Beginning Balance	50,415.00
Cleared Transactions	
Checks and Payments - 12 items	-2,983.00
Deposits and Credits - 1 item	1,500.00
Total Cleared Transactions	-1,483.00
Cleared Balance	48,932.00
Register Balance as of 12/31/2012	48,932.00
Ending Balance ▶	48,932.00 ◀

5. Close the Reconciliation Summary report.

ACCOUNTING CYCLE

Chapters 3-5 in this text work together to process the tasks in the accounting cycle for October through December. The steps of the Accounting Cycle that you do in this text are:

QuickBooks Accounting Cycle
1. Set up a company.
2. Record transactions.
3. Post entries automatically.
4. Account Reconciliation.
5. Print the Trial Balance (unadjusted).
6. Record and post adjusting entries.
7. Print the Trial Balance (adjusted).
8. Print the financial statements: balance sheet, profit and loss, cash flow statement.
9. Close the fiscal year.
10. Interpret accounting information.

At the end of December, which is also the end of the fiscal year, you complete the remaining tasks by printing an unadjusted trial balance, recording adjusting entries, printing financial statements, and closing the fiscal year.

UNADJUSTED TRIAL BALANCE

1. Print the 12/31/20XX Trial Balance (unadjusted). Compare your
    unadjusted trial balance to the one shown below.

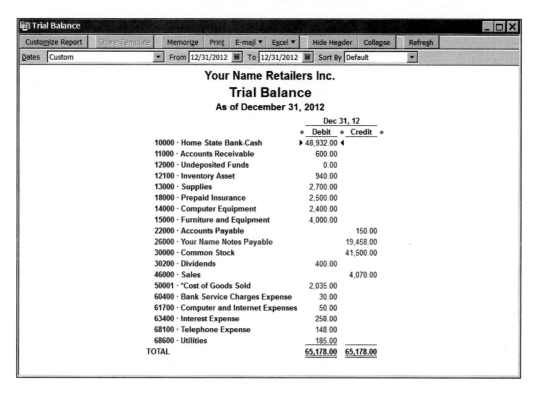

Trial Balance	Debit	Credit
10000 · Home State Bank-Cash	48,932.00	
11000 · Accounts Receivable	600.00	
12000 · Undeposited Funds	0.00	
12100 · Inventory Asset	940.00	
13000 · Supplies	2,700.00	
18000 · Prepaid Insurance	2,500.00	
14000 · Computer Equipment	2,400.00	
15000 · Furniture and Equipment	4,000.00	
22000 · Accounts Payable		150.00
26000 · Your Name Notes Payable		19,458.00
30000 · Common Stock		41,500.00
30200 · Dividends	400.00	
46000 · Sales		4,070.00
50001 · *Cost of Goods Sold	2,035.00	
60400 · Bank Service Charges Expense	30.00	
61700 · Computer and Internet Expenses	50.00	
63400 · Interest Expense	258.00	
68100 · Telephone Expense	148.00	
68600 · Utilities	185.00	
TOTAL	65,178.00	65,178.00

Your Name Retailers Inc.
Trial Balance
As of December 31, 2012
Dec 31, 12

2. Backup the company data through the unadjusted trial balance to
    your USB drive. Name your backup **Your Name Chapter 5
    December UTB** in the File name field. (*Hint:* UTB is an abbreviation
    of unadjusted trial balance.)

3. Exit QuickBooks or continue with the next section.

END-OF-QUARTER ADJUSTING ENTRIES

It is the policy of your company to record adjusting entries at the end of
the quarter to properly reflect all the quarter's business activities.

Follow these steps to record and post the adjusting entries in the journal.

1. From the Menu Bar, select Company; Make General Journal
    Entries.

2. When the Assigning Numbers to Journal Entries screen appears, read it and click [OK].

3. Make sure the box next to Adjusting Entry is checked [☑ Adjusting Entry]. When you check the Adjusting Entry box, adjusting entries are identified on QB reports.

4. If necessary, type **5** in the Entry No. field. That is the first adjusting entry number.

5. Type **12/31/20XX (use your current year)** in the Date field.

6. In the Account field, select the appropriate account to debit. (See transactions 1-5 below.)

7. Type the appropriate amount in the Debit field.

8. Select the appropriate account to credit. Make sure the Credit field shows the appropriate amount.

9. Click [Save & New] to go to the next journal entry.

The following adjusting entries need to be recorded. Record and post these December 31, 20XX adjusting entries:

1. Supplies on hand are $2,400.00. (This is Journal No. 5.)

Acct. #	Account Name	Debit	Credit
64900	Supplies Expense	300.00	
13000	Supplies		300.00

Computation:
Supplies	$2,700.00
Office supplies on hand	- 2,400.00
Adjustment	$ 300.00

(Hint: To post your transaction, click [Save & New] after each journal entry.)

2. Adjust three months of prepaid insurance $150.00 ($50 per month x 3 months). (This is Journal No. 6.)

Acct. #	Account Name	Debit	Credit
63300	Insurance Expense	150.00	
18000	Prepaid Insurance		150.00

3. Use straight-line depreciation for your computer equipment. Your computer equipment has a five-year service life and no salvage value. (Journal No. 7.)

To depreciate computer equipment for the fourth quarter, use this calculation:

$2,400 ÷ 5 years X 3/12 months = $120.00

Acct. #	Account Name	Debit	Credit
62400	Depreciation Expense	120.00	
16000	Accumulated Depreciation-CEqmt.		120.00

Read the Tracking Fixed Assets on Journal Entries window, then click OK.

4. Use straight-line depreciation to depreciate your furniture. The furniture has a 5-year service life and no salvage value. (Journal No. 8.)

To depreciate furniture for the fourth quarter, use this calculation:

$4,000 ÷ 5 years X 3/12 months = $200.00

Acct. #	Account Name	Debit	Credit
62400	Depreciation Expense	200.00	
17000	Accumulated Depreciation-F&E		200.00

Read the Tracking Fixed Assets on Journal Entries box, then click OK.

5.   After making the end-of-quarter adjusting entries, close the Make General Journal Entries window, then display the Adjusting Journal Entries for 12/31/20XX. (*Hint:* Report Center; Accountant & Taxes, Adjusting Journal Entries.) If you placed a check mark next to adjusting entries (step 3, page 182) on the Make General Journal Entries window, only adjusting entries will display.

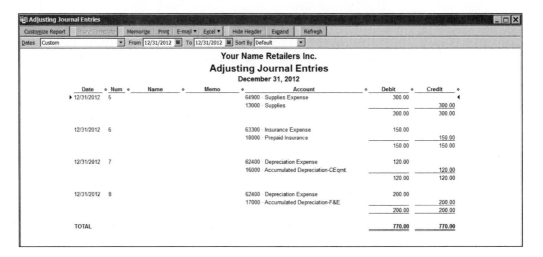

If your adjusting journal entries in the Journal do *not* agree with the Adjusting Journal Entries window, edit them.

6.   Close the Journal without saving.

7.   Print the 12/31/20XX Adjusted Trial Balance. Compare your adjusted trial balance to the one shown on the next page.

```
┌─────────────────────────────────────────────────────────────────────────────────┐
│ ▣ Adjusted Trial Balance                                                 _ □ ✕    │
├─────────────────────────────────────────────────────────────────────────────────┤
│ Customize Report  Share Template  Memorize  Print  E-mail ▼  Excel ▼  Hide Header │
│                                                              Collapse   Refresh    │
│ Dates  Custom            ▼  From 12/31/2012 ▥  To 12/31/2012 ▥  Sort By Default ▼  │
└─────────────────────────────────────────────────────────────────────────────────┘
```

Your Name Retailers Inc.
Adjusted Trial Balance
December 31, 2012

	Unadjusted Balance		Adjustments		Adjusted Balance	
	Debit	Credit	Debit	Credit	Debit	Credit
10000 · Home State Bank-Cash	▶ 48,932.00 ◀				48,932.00	
11000 · Accounts Receivable	600.00				600.00	
12000 · Undeposited Funds	0.00				0.00	
12100 · Inventory Asset	940.00				940.00	
13000 · Supplies	2,700.00			300.00	2,400.00	
18000 · Prepaid Insurance	2,500.00			150.00	2,350.00	
14000 · Computer Equipment	2,400.00				2,400.00	
15000 · Furniture and Equipment	4,000.00				4,000.00	
16000 · Accumulated Depreciation-CEqmt.				120.00		120.00
17000 · Accumulated Depreciation-F&E				200.00		200.00
22000 · Accounts Payable		150.00				150.00
26000 · Your Name Notes Payable		19,458.00				19,458.00
30000 · Common Stock		41,500.00				41,500.00
30200 · Dividends	400.00				400.00	
46000 · Sales		4,070.00				4,070.00
50001 · *Cost of Goods Sold	2,035.00				2,035.00	
60400 · Bank Service Charges Expense	30.00				30.00	
61700 · Computer and Internet Expenses	50.00				50.00	
62400 · Depreciation Expense			320.00		320.00	
63300 · Insurance Expense			150.00		150.00	
63400 · Interest Expense	258.00				258.00	
64900 · Supplies Expense			300.00		300.00	
68100 · Telephone Expense	148.00				148.00	
68600 · Utilities	185.00				185.00	
TOTAL	65,178.00	65,178.00	770.00	770.00	65,498.00	65,498.00

8. Print the 10/01/20XX to 12/31/20XX Profit and Loss-Standard (income statement). Compare yours to the one shown on the next page.

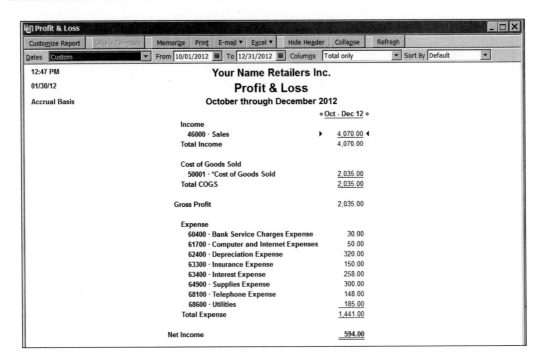

9.   Print the 12/31/20XX Balance Sheet-Standard. Compare yours to the one shown on the next page.

Your Name Retailers Inc.
Balance Sheet
As of December 31, 2012

	◇ Dec 31, 12 ◇
ASSETS	
Current Assets	
Checking/Savings	
10000 · Home State Bank-Cash	▶ 48,932.00 ◀
Total Checking/Savings	48,932.00
Accounts Receivable	
11000 · Accounts Receivable	600.00
Total Accounts Receivable	600.00
Other Current Assets	
12100 · Inventory Asset	940.00
13000 · Supplies	2,400.00
18000 · Prepaid Insurance	2,350.00
Total Other Current Assets	5,690.00
Total Current Assets	55,222.00
Fixed Assets	
14000 · Computer Equipment	2,400.00
15000 · Furniture and Equipment	4,000.00
16000 · Accumulated Depreciation-CEqmt.	-120.00
17000 · Accumulated Depreciation-F&E	-200.00
Total Fixed Assets	6,080.00
TOTAL ASSETS	**61,302.00**
LIABILITIES & EQUITY	
Liabilities	
Current Liabilities	
Accounts Payable	
22000 · Accounts Payable	150.00
Total Accounts Payable	150.00
Total Current Liabilities	150.00
Long Term Liabilities	
26000 · Your Name Notes Payable	19,458.00
Total Long Term Liabilities	19,458.00
Total Liabilities	19,608.00
Equity	
30000 · Common Stock	41,500.00
30200 · Dividends	-400.00
Net Income	594.00
Total Equity	41,694.00
TOTAL LIABILITIES & EQUITY	**61,302.00**

10. Print the 10/01/20XX to 12/31/20XX Statement of Cash Flows.

Your Name Retailers Inc.
Statement of Cash Flows
October through December 2012

	◊ Oct - Dec 12 ◊
OPERATING ACTIVITIES	
Net Income	▶ 594.00 ◀
Adjustments to reconcile Net Income	
to net cash provided by operations:	
11000 · Accounts Receivable	-600.00
12100 · Inventory Asset	-940.00
13000 · Supplies	100.00
18000 · Prepaid Insurance	150.00
22000 · Accounts Payable	150.00
Net cash provided by Operating Activities	-546.00
INVESTING ACTIVITIES	
14000 · Computer Equipment	-1,400.00
16000 · Accumulated Depreciation-CEqmt.	120.00
17000 · Accumulated Depreciation-F&E	200.00
Net cash provided by Investing Activities	-1,080.00
FINANCING ACTIVITIES	
26000 · Your Name Notes Payable	-542.00
30000 · Common Stock	1,500.00
30200 · Dividends	-400.00
Net cash provided by Financing Activities	558.00
Net cash increase for period	-1,068.00
Cash at beginning of period	50,000.00
Cash at end of period	48,932.00

Comment

If your statement of cash flows or other financial statements *do not agree* with the textbook illustrations, drill-down to the appropriate entries. Edit the entries, then post and reprint your reports.

---

11. Backup. The suggested file name is **Your Name Chapter 5 December Financial Statements**.

CLOSING THE FISCAL YEAR

When you close the fiscal year, all revenue and expense accounts are moved to Account No. 32000, Retained Earnings. Moving the expense and revenue accounts to retained earnings is called ***closing the fiscal year***. The Dividends account must also be closed to Retained Earnings.

Follow these steps to close Dividends and close the fiscal year.

1. From the menu bar, select Company, Make General Journal Entries (Journal Entry 9). When the Assigning Numbers to Journal Entries window appears, click [OK]. Make sure the Adjusting Entry box is unchecked.

    Make the following December 31, 20XX closing entry for dividends.

Acct. #	Account Name	Debit	Credit
32000	Retained Earnings	400.00	
30200	Dividends		400.00

2. Compare your entry to the one below. When satisfied, click [Save & Close].

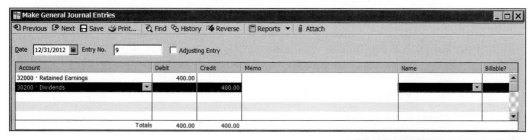

3. When the Retained Earnings warning screen appears, read it and then click [OK].

4. From the menu bar, select Company; Set Closing Date.

5.   The Preferences window appears.

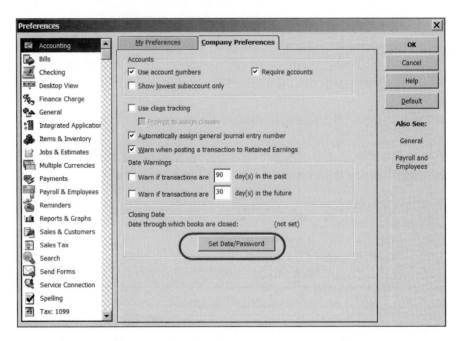

6.   Click [Set Date/Password]. The Set Closing Date and Password window appears. For Closing Date, type **12/31/20XX** (use your current year). **Do not type a password!** Click [OK].

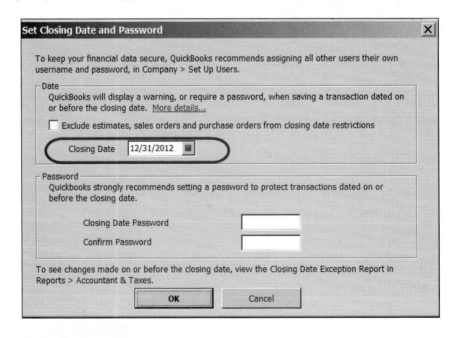

7. When the No Password Entered window appears, read it. Then, click [No]. Click [OK] to close the Preferences window.

PRINTING THE POSTCLOSING TRIAL BALANCE

After the fiscal year is closed, a postclosing trial balance is displayed and printed. Observe that the postclosing trial balance does *not* show dividends, revenue and expense accounts.

1. Display the 01/01/20YY (use the year after your current year) trial balance. (*Hint:* From the menu bar, select Reports; Accountant & Taxes, Trial Balance.) Compare yours to the one below, when satisfied, print your postclosing trial balance.

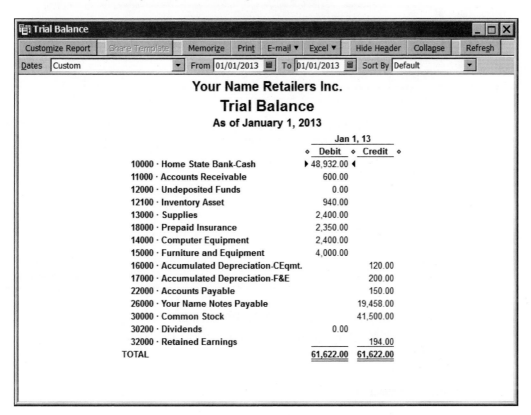

Notice Retained Earnings has a credit balance of $194.00 since the company's net income was greater than the dividends paid.

2. Close the postclosing trial balance without saving.

BACKUP END-OF-YEAR DATA

1. Back up the data through year end to your USB drive. The suggested file name is **Your Name Chapter 5 EOY (Portable).QBM**. (*Hint:* EOY is an abbreviation of end of year.) Since you are going to email this file to your instructor, use the portable file format—File; Create Copy, Portable company file.

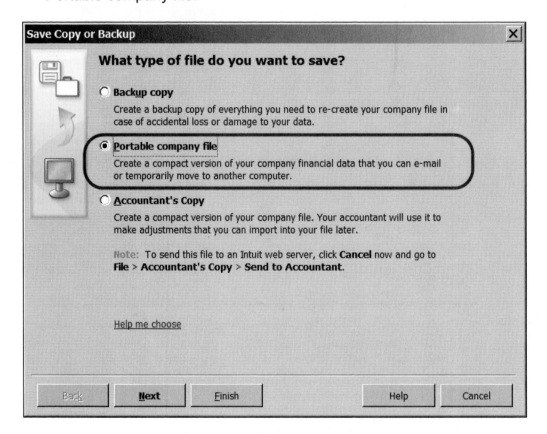

Portable company files create a compact version of your data. Files ending in a QBM extension are smaller than backups that have a .QBB file extension.

2. Exit QuickBooks or continue with the next section.

ACCOUNTANT TRANSFER

At year-end, external accountants or auditors review a company's accounting records. In this text, the external accountant is your professor. It is time to send your end-of-year portable company file via e-mail to you professor.

1.   Start your e-mail program.

2.   Create an e-mail message to your professor. Type **Your Name Retailers EOY** for the Subject. (Use your first and last name)

3.   Attach the portable backup file **Your Name Chapter 5 EOY (Portable)** that you made on the previous page to your instructor.

4.   CC yourself on the message to be sure the message sends properly.

5.   Send the message to your professor. You should receive a copy of it as well.

SUMMARY AND REVIEW

OBJECTIVES:

1.   Restore data from the Exercise 4-2.
2.   Record a compound journal entry.
3.   Write checks for expenses.
4.   Make deposits.
5.   Complete account reconciliation.
6.   Print the trial balance (unadjusted).
7.   Record and post quarterly adjusting entries in the General Journal.
8.   Print adjusted trial balance and financial statements.
9.   Close the fiscal year.
10.   Print a Postclosing Trial Balance.
11.   Make backups of Chapter 5 data.

Additional textbook related resources are on the textbook website at www.mhhe.com/QBessentials2012. It includes chapter resources, including troubleshooting tips, online quizzes, etc.

RESOURCEFUL QUICKBOOKS

Use the QuickBooks Learning Center (Help; Learning Center Tutorials) to answer the following questions. Link to What's New. View the What's New in QuickBooks 2012 video then answer these questions:

1. What is the Calendar view? Where do you see past-due notices?

2. How does the "To Do's" feature work with the calendar?

3. What does the one-click credit memo feature do? What button do you select on the original invoice to create a credit memo?

Multiple Choice questions: The Online Learning Center includes the multiple-choice questions at www.mhhe.com/QBessentials2012, select Student Edition, Chapter 5, Multiple Choice.

_____1. Compound entries affect at least how many accounts?

    a. One.
    b. Two.
    c. Three.
    d. None of the above.

_____2. Write checks icon is found in which pane on the Home page:

    a. Banking.
    b. Customers.
    c. Company.
    d. Vendors.

_____3. The Check Register displays information about:

    a. Deposits.
    b. Checks.
    c. Cash balance.
    d. All of the above.

_____4. An account reconciliation is completed:

    a. When the bank statement is received.
    b. Daily.
    c. Weekly.
    d. Annually.

_____5. The correct order of Accounting Cycle steps is:

    a. Record entries, Print the adjusted trial balance, Record and post adjusting entries, Close the fiscal year.
    b. Record and post adjusting entries, Account reconciliation, Print the unadjusted trial balance, Close the fiscal year.
    c. Record entries, Print the unadjusted trial balance, Record and post adjusting entries, Close the fiscal year.
    d. Record entries, Print the adjusted trial balance, Account reconciliation, Close the fiscal year.

_____6. The adjusting entry for depreciation is:

    a. Debit Accumulated Depreciation account and Credit Depreciation Expense account.
    b. Debit Depreciation Expense account and Credit Accumulated Depreciation account.
    c. Debit Computer Equipment account and Credit Accumulated Depreciation account.
    d. Debit Depreciation Expense account and Credit Computer Equipment.

_____7. Make General Journal Entries window is used to record:

    a. Compound entries.
    b. Adjusting entries.
    c. Closing entries.
    d. All of the above.

_____8. Financial statements are prepared in the following order:

   a. Balance Sheet, Income Statement, and Statement of Cash Flow.
   b. Statement of Cash Flow, Income Statement, and Balance Sheet.
   c. Income Statement, Balance Sheet, and Statement of Cash Flow.
   d. Balance Sheet, Statement of Cash Flow, and Income Statement.

_____9. Closing entries move the following account balances to Retained Earnings at the end of the fiscal year:

   a. Revenue and expense accounts.
   b. Dividend and liability accounts.
   c. Expense and asset accounts.
   d. Asset and liability accounts.

_____10. Postclosing Trial Balance contains:

   a. Only statement of cash flow accounts.
   b. No revenue, expense, or dividend accounts.
   c. Only profit and loss accounts.
   d. Only stockholders' equity accounts.

Short-answer questions: To answer these questions, go online to www.mhhe.com/QBessentials2012, link to Student Edition, Chapter 5, QA Templates. The analysis question at the end of the chapter is also included.

1. Define a compound transaction.

2. What is the account distribution for the note payable payment?

3. What account is debited to pay dividends? What account is credited?

4. What account is debited to pay for cellular phone service? What account is credited?

5.   What account is debited to pay for Internet service? What account is credited?

6.   What account is debited to pay for water and garbage? What account is credited?

7.   What is the check register and what does it show?

8.   In Chapter 5 what steps of the accounting cycle did you complete?

9.   Why does Your Name Retailers Inc. make adjusting journal entries?

10. What accounts never appear in a company's postclosing trial balance?

Exercise 5-1: Follow the instructions below to complete Exercise 5-1.

1.   If necessary start QuickBooks and open Your Name Retailers.

2.   Print the Audit Trail report for All dates. (*HINT:* Report Center; Accountant & Taxes, Audit Trail.)

 Read me: Audit Trail

When changes are made to a transaction, the Num column is shown in italics; the State column shows Latest and Prior. If the amount was changed, it is shown in boldface.

---

3.   Your instructor may want you to email the Audit Trial report as a PDF attachment. To do that, display the Audit Trail report (all dates), then select File; Save as PDF. (*Hint:* There is also an E-mail button on the Audit Trial's icon bar. Select E-mail, then send the

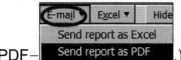

report as a PDF—.) The suggested file name is **Chapter 5 Audit Trail.pdf**.

Exercise 5-2: Answer the questions in the space provided? Use the following abbreviations to identify reports: IS (income statement); BS (balance sheet); CFS (cash flow statement).

1. What report(s) show the net income or net loss? _____

2. What report(s) show the cash balance? _____

3. What report(s) show total fixed assets? _____

4. What report(s) show common stock? _____

5. What reports(s) show cash at the beginning of the period? _____

6. What report(s) show note payable accounts? _____

7. What report(s) show total expenses? _____

8. What report(s) show the gross profit? _____

9. What report(s) show cost of goods sold? _____

10. What report(s) show retained earnings? _____

ANALYSIS QUESTION:

How is the December 31, 20XX retained earnings balance computed? Show the computation.

Chapter 6

First Month of the New Year

OBJECTIVES:

1. Restore data from Your Name Chapter 5 EOY file.
2. Record one month of transactions.
3. Make bank deposit.
4. Complete account reconciliation.
5. Print a trial balance (unadjusted).
6. Record adjusting entries and print an adjusted trial balance.
7. Print financial statements.
8. Make backups of Chapter 6 data.[1]

Additional textbook related resources are on the textbook website at www.mhhe.com/QBessentials2012. It includes chapter resources, including online quizzes, etc.

GETTING STARTED:

1. Start QuickBooks. Open Your Name Retailers Inc.

2. If necessary, open/restore the Your Name Chapter 5 EOY. This backup was made in the previous chapter.

3. To make sure you are starting in the correct place, display the 01/01/20YY (20YY is the year after your current year, i.e., if your current year is 2012, use 2013 for year 20YY) trial balance.

   Compare your trial balance with the one shown on the next page. The January 1, 20YY postclosing trial balance is also shown on page 191.

---

[1]The chart in the Preface, page xii, shows the files names and size of each backup file. Refer to this chart for backing up data. Remember, you can back up to a hard drive location or external media.

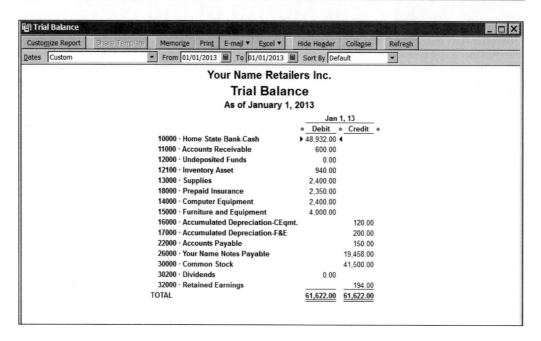

4. Close the trial balance.

In this chapter you will apply what you have learned in this text to complete steps 2-8 in the accounting cycle for January. Remember the steps in the accounting cycle include:

Accounting Cycle
1. Set up a company.
2. Record transactions.
3. Post entries.
4. Account Reconciliation.
5. Print the Trial Balance (unadjusted).
6. Record and post adjusting entries.
7. Print the Trial Balance (adjusted).
8. Print the financial statements: balance sheet, profit and loss, cash flow statement.
9. Close the fiscal year.
10. Interpret accounting information.

RECORD FIRST MONTH OF NEW FISCAL YEAR TRANSACTIONS

Record the following transactions from your Check Register for the month of January 20YY (20YY is the year after your current year, i.e., if your current year is 2012, use 2013 for year 20YY):

Write Checks

Check Number	Date	Description of Transaction	Payment	Deposit	Balance
					48,932.00
4021	1/3	The Business Store (Acct.15000, Furniture and Equipment) for computer furniture	500.00		48,432.00
4022	1/4	The Office Supply Store (Acct. No. 13000, Supplies)	100.00		48,332.00

Record the following vendor and customer transactions for the month of January:

Date   *Description of Transaction*

1/05   Enter bill (Invoice No. 201PS) for items received from Podcast Ltd. for the purchase of 30 audio files, $15 each, for a total of $450.

1/05   Enter bill (Invoice No. 150eB) for items received from eBooks Express for the purchase of 32 PDF files, $25 each, for a total of $800.

1/05   Invoice No. 400TV received from TV Flix for the purchase of 30 video files, $30 each, for a total of $900.

1/10   Returned two PDF files to eBooks Express Credit Memo No. CM3, $50.

1/15   Create invoice to sell 10 eBooks (PDF files) on account to iPrint Design for a total credit sale of $500, Invoice # 9.

1/15   Create invoice to sell 30 Podcasts (audio files) on account to Audio Answers for a total credit sale of $900, Invoice # 10.

1/15	Sold 16 TV Programs (video files) on account to Video Solutions for a total credit sale of $960, Invoice # 11.
1/17	Audio Answers returned 2 Podcasts (audio files), $60, Credit No. 12. Apply to 1/15 invoice.
1/18	Create sales receipt (Sale No. 3) for credit card sales for 10 eBooks for $500; 1 Podcasts for $30; and 12 TV Programs for $720; for total credit card sales of $1,250.
1/20	Received a $600 check from Video Solutions in payment of 12/24 credit sale less return.
1/20	Your Name Retailers Inc. pays all outstanding December and January vendor bills less any returns for a total of $2,250. (*HINT:* eBooks Express $50 credit)
1/21	Enter bill to purchase computer furniture on account from The Business Store, Invoice BOS80, for a total of $800, terms Net 30 days. (Account No. 15000 Furniture and Equipment)
1/23	Received a check in full payment of Audio Answers' account less return, $840.
1/24	Received a check in full payment of iPrint Design's account, $500.
1/24	Received a check in full payment of Video Solution's account, $960.
1/25	Enter bill (Invoice No. 175eB) received from eBooks Express for the purchase of 8 PDF files, $25 each, for a total of $200.
1/25	Invoice No. 425TV received from TV Flix for the purchase of 11 video files, $30 each, for a total of $330.
1/25	Invoice No. 230PS received from Podcast Ltd. for the purchase of 6 audio files, $15 each, for a total of $90.

1/26   Returned two audio files to Podcast Ltd., CM4, $30.

1/27   Create invoice to sell 16 eBooks (PDF files) on account to
              iPrint Design for a total credit sale of $800, Invoice # 13.

1/27   Sold 5 Podcasts (audio files) on account to Audio Answers
              for a total credit sale of $150 Invoice # 14.

1/27   Sold 6 TV Programs (video files) on account to Video
              Solutions for a total credit sale of $360, Invoice # 15.

1/27   Enter sales receipt for credit card sales. Sold 2 eBooks for
              $100; 1 Podcasts for $30; and 6 TV Programs for $360; for
              total credit card sales of $490, Sale No. 4.

1/28   Video Solutions returned 1 TV Programs (video files),
              Credit No. 16. Apply $60 credit to 1/27 invoice.

1/29   Received a check in full payment of Audio Answers'
              account, $150.

1/29   Received a check in full payment of iPrint Design's account,
              $800.

1/29   Your Name Retailers Inc. pays all outstanding vendor bills
              less any returns for a total of $1,390. (*Hint:* Podcast Ltd.
              $30 credit.)

Record the following compound entry for the month of January: (*HINT:*
Company; Make General Journal Entries)

1/30   Pay the note payable in the amount of $800.00. The
              account distribution is:

Acct. No.	Account	Debit	Credit
26000	Your Name Note Payable	555.00	
63400	Interest Expense	245.00	
10000	Home State Bank-Cash		800.00

Write checks for these additional January transactions.

1/30	Issue Check No. 4031 to Mobile One in the amount of $80 for cellular service. (Account No. 68100 Telephone Expense)
1/30	Issue Check No. 4032 to ISP in the amount of $50 for Internet service. (Account No. 61700 Computer and Internet Expense)
1/30	Issue Check No. 4033 to Everywhere Telephone Service in the amount of $68 for telephone service. (Account No. 68100 Telephone Expense)
1/30	Issue Check No. 4034 to Reno Water/Garbage in the amount of $111 for Electricity/Gas. (Account No. 68600 Utilities.)
1/30	Issue Check No. 4035 to Reno Water/Garbage for $74 for Water/Garbage service. (Account No. 68600 Utilities).
1/30	View the Check Register. Select Check 4034, then click [✎ Edit Transaction]. The Write Checks window appears for the disbursement. Check No. 4034 should be written to Regional Utilities, not Reno Water/Garbage. Write the check correctly to Regional Utilities to pay $111 electricity bill. (*HINT:* Use Payee pulldown menu.) Close the Write Checks window and the Check Register.

MAKE DEPOSIT

1/30	Record 8 deposits in the amount of $5,590. This includes payments received from customers and credit card sales.

CHECK REGISTER

Display the check register to see Account No. 10000, Home State Bank-Cash activity for January. Compare to one shown on the next page. If necessary, select the check that needs to be changed, then select [✎ Edit Transaction] to go to the Write Checks window.

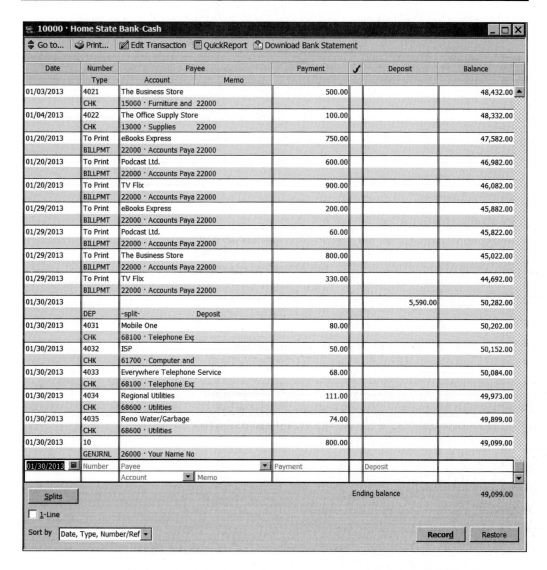

Backup. The suggested file name is **Your Name Chapter 6 January Check Register.QBB**. (If a screen appears that says number of backup copies has been exceeded, click No, don't delete.)

ACCOUNT RECONCILIATION

Use the January bank statement on the next page to reconcile the Home State Bank account. Checks numbers are shown on the following bank statement. Depending on whether you recorded a check number for each vendor payment, check numbers may or may not be included on the Reconcile window.

Statement of Account Home State Bank January 1 to January 31, 20YY Account #0618-3201			Your Name Retailers Inc. Your Address Reno, NV	
REGULAR CHECKING				
Previous Balance	12/31	48,932.00		
Deposits		5,590.00		
Checks (-)		5,423.00		
Service Charges (-)	1/31	10.00		
Ending Balance	1/31	**$49,089.00**		
DEPOSITS				
	1/18	1,250.00	Credit Card	
	1/27	490.00	Credit Card	
	1/30	600.00	Video Solutions	
	1/30	840.00	Audio Answers	
	1/30	500.00	iPrint Design	
	1/30	960.00	Video Solutions	
	1/30	150.00	Audio Answers	
	1/30	800.00	iPrint Design	
CHECKS				
	1/4	500.00	4021	
	1/4	100.00	4022	
	1/22	750.00	4023	
	1/22	600.00	4024	
	1/22	900.00	4025	
	1/30	800.00	4026	
	1/30	200.00	4027	
	1/30	60.00	4028	
	1/30	330.00	4029	
	1/31	800.00	4030	
	1/31	80.00	4031	
	1/31	50.00	4032	
	1/31	68.00	4033	
	1/31	111.00	4034	
	1/31	74.00	4035	

Once the $10 Service Charge is deducted from the account register balance, the bank statement and account register agree.

Check Register Balance:	$49,099.00
Bank Service Charge:	10.00
Bank Statement Balance:	$49,089.00

1.   Prepare the account reconciliation for January.

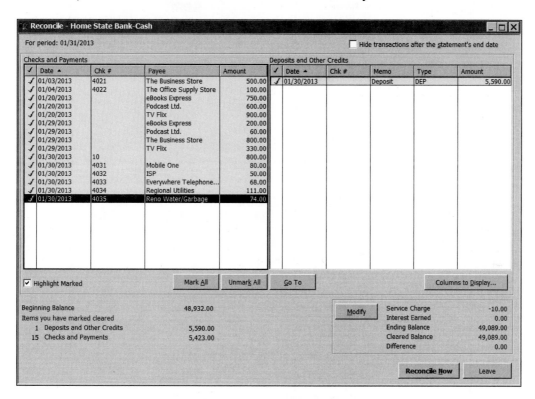

Hint: Your Reconcile window may not show all of the check numbers. That is okay.

2.   Display the Reconciliation Summary report. Compare yours to the one shown on the next page.

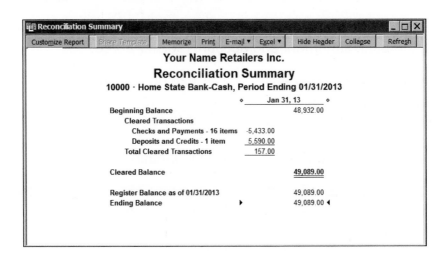

UNADJUSTED TRIAL BALANCE

1. Print the 1/31/20YY Trial Balance (unadjusted). Compare your unadjusted trial balance to the one shown below.

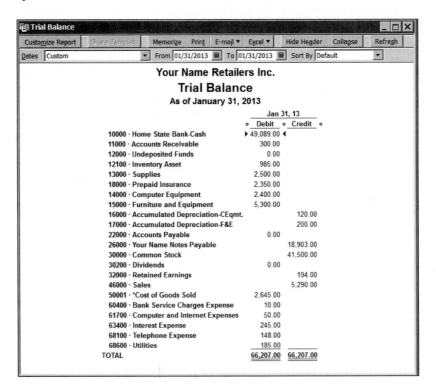

2. Backup. The suggested file name is **Your Name Chapter 6 UTB**.

Troubleshooting: If a Delete Extra Backups window appears, select [No, Don't Delete].

> **Delete Extra Backups?**
>
> The option that limits the number of backup copies you can save manually in each folder is set to 3. The backup copy you're saving now brings the number of manually saved backups to 5. Is it OK to delete the 2 oldest backup(s) now?
>
> [**Yes, Delete**]   (**No, Don't Delete**)

To increase the number of backups to a folder, do this:

1. Go to the File menu, click Create Backup.
2. Select the <Options> button.
3. If needed, Browse to your preferred backup location.
4. In the Limit the number of backup copies in this folder to, type **20**. Press <Tab>.

☑ Limit the number of backup copies in this folder to [20] . Click <OK>.

5. Close the Create Backup window.

END-OF-MONTH ADJUSTING ENTRIES

Your Name Retailers Inc. changed their adjusting entry policy for the new fiscal year. The new policy is to record adjusting entries at the end of each month to properly reflect all the month's business activities. Make the following adjusting entries for the month of January on 01/31/20YY. (*HINT:* Company, Make General Journal Entries, check mark next to Adjusting Entry— ☑ Adjusting Entry .)

1. Supplies on hand are $2,300.00. (This is Entry No. 11.)

Acct. #	Account Name	Debit	Credit
64900	Supplies Expense	200.00	
13000	Supplies		200.00

Computation: Supplies $2,500.00
                 Office supplies on hand   - 2,300.00
                 Adjustment $ 200.00

2. Adjust one month of prepaid insurance ($50/month). (Entry No. 12.)

Acct. #	Account Name	Debit	Credit
63300	Insurance Expense	50.00	
18000	Prepaid Insurance		50.00

3. Use straight-line depreciation for your computer equipment. Your computer equipment has a five-year service life and no salvage value. (Entry No. 13.)

   To depreciate computer equipment for the month, use this calculation: $2,400 ÷ 5 years X 1/12 months = $40.00

Acct. #	Account Name	Debit	Credit
62400	Depreciation Expense	40.00	
16000	Accumulated Depreciation-CEqmt.		40.00

4. Use straight-line depreciation to depreciate furniture. The furniture has a 5-year service life and no salvage value. (Entry No. 14.) To depreciate furniture for the month, use this calculation: $4,000 ÷ 5 years X 1/12 month = $67.00

Acct. #	Account Name	Debit	Credit
62400	Depreciation Expense	67.00	
17000	Accumulated Depreciation-F&E		67.00

5. You purchased new furniture during the month. Use straight-line depreciation to depreciate your furniture. The furniture has a 5-year service life and a $100 salvage value.

   Use the following adjusting entry. (Entry No. 15.) The computation is: ($500 + $800 -$100)÷ 5 years X 1/12 month = $20.00

Acct. #	Account Name	Debit	Credit
62400	Depreciation Expense	20.00	
17000	Accumulated Depreciation-F&E		20.00

6. After journalizing and posting the adjusting entries, close the Make General Journal Entries window, then display or print the Adjusting Journal Entries as of 01/31/20YY. If your Journal does *not* agree with the one shown, drilldown on error to edit and correct.

Comment: If your unadjusted and adjusted trial balances *do not agree* with the textbook illustration, drill-down to the appropriate entries. Edit the entries, then reprint your reports.

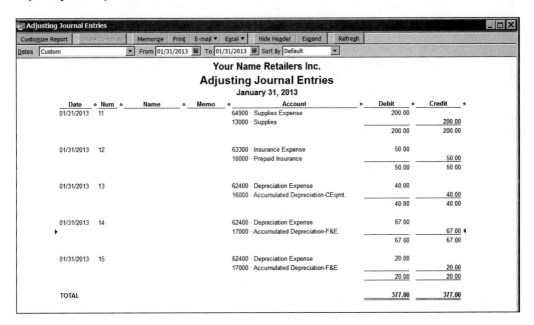

7. Close the Adjusting Journal Entries window without saving.

ADJUSTED TRIAL BALANCE

1. Print the 1/31/20YY Adjusted Trial Balance.

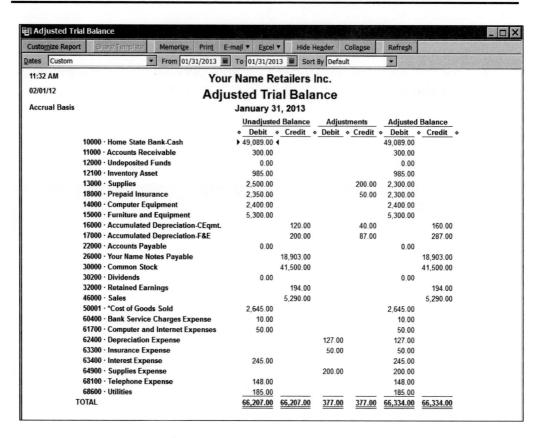

| Adjusted Trial Balance | | | | | | | |

11:32 AM
02/01/12
Accrual Basis

Your Name Retailers Inc.
Adjusted Trial Balance
January 31, 2013

	Unadjusted Balance Debit	Unadjusted Balance Credit	Adjustments Debit	Adjustments Credit	Adjusted Balance Debit	Adjusted Balance Credit
10000 · Home State Bank-Cash	49,089.00				49,089.00	
11000 · Accounts Receivable	300.00				300.00	
12000 · Undeposited Funds	0.00				0.00	
12100 · Inventory Asset	985.00				985.00	
13000 · Supplies	2,500.00			200.00	2,300.00	
18000 · Prepaid Insurance	2,350.00			50.00	2,300.00	
14000 · Computer Equipment	2,400.00				2,400.00	
15000 · Furniture and Equipment	5,300.00				5,300.00	
16000 · Accumulated Depreciation-CEqmt.		120.00		40.00		160.00
17000 · Accumulated Depreciation-F&E		200.00		87.00		287.00
22000 · Accounts Payable	0.00				0.00	
26000 · Your Name Notes Payable		18,903.00				18,903.00
30000 · Common Stock		41,500.00				41,500.00
30200 · Dividends	0.00				0.00	
32000 · Retained Earnings		194.00				194.00
46000 · Sales		5,290.00				5,290.00
50001 · *Cost of Goods Sold	2,645.00				2,645.00	
60400 · Bank Service Charges Expense	10.00				10.00	
61700 · Computer and Internet Expenses	50.00				50.00	
62400 · Depreciation Expense			127.00		127.00	
63300 · Insurance Expense			50.00		50.00	
63400 · Interest Expense	245.00				245.00	
64900 · Supplies Expense			200.00		200.00	
68100 · Telephone Expense	148.00				148.00	
68600 · Utilities	185.00				185.00	
TOTAL	66,207.00	66,207.00	377.00	377.00	66,334.00	66,334.00

2. Close the Adjusted Trial Balance, then backup. The suggested file name is **Your Name Chapter 6 January Financial Statements.QBB**.

3. Exit QuickBooks or continue with the next section.

SUMMARY AND REVIEW

OBJECTIVES:

1.   Restore data from Your Name Chapter 5 EOY.
2.   Record one month of transactions.
3.   Make bank deposit.
4.   Complete account reconciliation.
5.   Print a trial balance (unadjusted).
6.   Record adjusting entries and print an adjusted trial balance.
7.   Print financial statements.
8.   Make backups of Chapter 6 data.

Additional textbook related resources are on the textbook website at www.mhhe.com/QBessentials2012. It includes chapter resources, including troubleshooting tips, online quizzes, etc.

RESOURCEFUL QUICKBOOKS

1.   Click on Menu Bar Help; Year-End Guide, what are the three task areas that must be addressed at year-end? List them.

2.   Click on menu bar's Help; Support, or go online to http://support.quickbooks.intuit.com/support/.

     Select the Intuit Communities tab. Scroll down the page. Then, in the More Resources area, select Library. The URL is http://community.intuit.com/library. List resources found in the QB library.

Multiple Choice Questions: The Online Learning Center includes the multiple-choice questions at www.mhhe.com/QBessentials2012, select Student Edition, Chapter 6, Multiple Choice.

_____1. The January 1, 20YY Trial Balance contains:

    a. The same accounts as the 12/31/20XX post closing trial balance.
    b. No revenue, expense, or dividend accounts.
    c. Both of the above.
    d. None of the above.

_____2. In Chapter 6, you enter transactions for:

    a. The first month of the new fiscal year.
    b. January.
    c. Both of the above.
    d. None of the above.

_____3. In Chapter 6, you complete which steps in the Accounting Cycle?

    a. Steps 1.-9.
    b. Steps 2.-8.
    c. Steps 3.-7.
    d. All the steps.

_____4. In Chapter 6, all the following Home page Banking pane icons were used _except_:

    a. Reconcile.
    b. Check register.
    c. Write checks.
    d. Enter bills.

_____5. In Chapter 6, all the following Home page Customer pane icons were used _except_:

    a. Create invoices.
    b. Estimates.
    c. Create sales receipts.
    d. Receive payments.

_____6. In Chapter 6, the following Home page Vendor pane icon was used:

    a. Pay bills.
    b. Purchase Orders.
    c. Enter bills against inventory.
    d. Write bills.

_____7. In Chapter 6, the following Home page Company pane icon was used:

    a. Chart of accounts.
    b. Items and services.
    c. Both of the above.
    d. None of the above.

_____8. Learning Center Tutorials include all of the following _except_:

    a. Customers & Sales.
    b. Vendors & Expenses.
    c. Account Balances.
    d. Inventory.

_____9. The correct work flow path on the QuickBooks Home page for invoicing is:

    a. Create invoice, Receive payment, Record deposit.
    b. Create sales receipt, record deposit.
    c. Enter bill, Pay bill.
    d. Receive invoice, Pay bill.

_____10. The QuickBooks menu bar Help selection includes:

    a. Ask Intuit.
    b. Support.
    c. Year-end guide.
    d. All of the above.

Short-answer and True/make true questions: To answer these questions, go online to www.mhhe.com/QBessentials2012, link to Student Edition, Chapter 6, QA Templates. The analysis question at the end of the chapter is also included.

1. Your Name Retailers Inc. fiscal year begins on January 1.

2. Step 4 of the accounting cycle is reconciling the bank statement.

3. The check register's balance does *not* show the bank service charge.

4. Your check register and bank statement are used as source documents for recording entries.

5. In this chapter, Your Name Retailers Inc. makes adjusting journal entries on a quarterly basis.

6. In this chapter, accounting records are completed for January 1 - March 31, 20YY.

7. Your Name Retailers Inc. makes closing journal entries on a monthly basis.

8. For the period of January 1 to January 31, 20YY, Your Name Retailers Inc. net income (loss) is $_____.

9. At the end of the month, Your Name Retailers Inc. total assets are $_____.

10. At the end of the month, Your Name Retailers Inc. total liabilities are $_____.

11. At the end of the month, Your Name Retailers Inc. had generated cash flow from/for operating activities of $_____.

12. At the end of the month, Your Name Retailers Inc. had generated cash flow from/for financing activities of $_____.

Exercise 6-1: Follow the instructions below to complete Exercise 6-1.

1.   If necessary, start QB and open Your Name Retailers Inc.

2.   If necessary, restore the Your Name Chapter 6 January Financial Statements file. This backup was made on page 212.

3.   Back up the file as a portable company file. (*Hint:* File; Create Cop, Portable Company File.) The suggested file name is **Your Name Exercise 6-1 (Portable).QBM**.

4.   Print the 01/01/20YY to 01/31/20YY Journal.

5.   Print the 01/31/20YY trial balance.

6.   Print the financial statements:

     a. Profit & Loss-Standard from 01/01/20YY to 01/31/20YY).

     b. Balance Sheet-Standard as of 01/31/20YY.

     c. Statement of Cash Flows from 01/01/20YY to 01/31/20YY.

7.   Print the Audit Trail for all dates.

   Read Me: Save reports as PDF Files

Your instructor may want you to email reports as PDF attachments. To do that, follow these steps:

1.   Display the report.
2.   From the menu bar, select File; Save as PDF. *Or,* click the report's E-mail button and select Send reports as PDF.
3.   The suggested file name is **Exercise 6-1 Journal.pdf**, etc.

You need Adobe Reader to save as PDF files. If download the free Adobe Reader, www.adobe.com.

Exercise 6-2:

Send an e-mail to your professor and attach a copy of Your Name Exercise 6-1 (Portable).QBM file. (*HINT:* Follow the Accountant Transfer steps 1-5 in Chapter 5.)

ANALYSIS QUESTION:

Why did Your Name Retailers Inc. generate more cash from operating activities than net income for January?

<table>
<tr><td>**Project**
1</td><td># Your Name Hardware Store</td></tr>
</table>

In Project 1, you complete the business processes for Your Name Hardware Store, a merchandising business. Your Name Hardware Store sells shovels, wagons, and wheel barrows. It is organized as a corporation. The purpose of Project 1 is to review what you have learned about merchandising businesses and use their typical source documents. Source documents that trigger transaction analysis for accounts payable, inventory, accounts receivable, and cash are included in this project. You will also prepare a bank reconciliation. A checklist is shown listing the printed reports that should be completed at the end of this project. The step-by-step instructions also remind you to print reports and backup at regular intervals.

GETTING STARTED

Follow these steps to open Your Name Hardware Store:

Step 1: Start QuickBooks 2012. From the menu bar, select File; Close Company.

Step 2: The No Company Open window appears. Restore the backup file, Your Name Hardware Store.QBB. Rename the company file Your Name Project 1 Begin.qbw. (*HINT:* You created this company and backed it up in Exercise 1-2, page 26. If the Your Name Hardware Store.QBB backup file does <u>not</u> exist, complete Exercises 1-1 and 1-2 on page 26.)

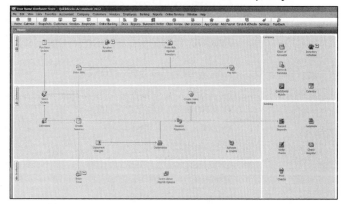

Step 3:   Confirm company information. From Menu Bar select Company; Company Information. Compare your screen to the one shown here. (*Hint:* Your first and last name should be shown before Hardware Store.)

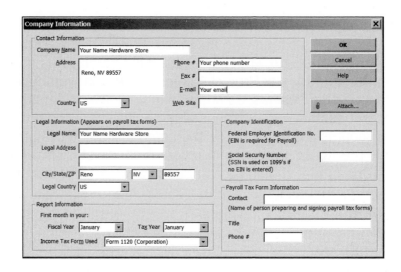

Step 4:   When satisfied that company information is correct, click OK.

COMPANY PREFERENCES

Step 5:   From the menu bar, select Edit; Preferences. Click on Company Preferences tab and select Accounting.

Step 6:   Click on the box next to Use account numbers. Make sure boxes next to Date warnings are unchecked then click OK.

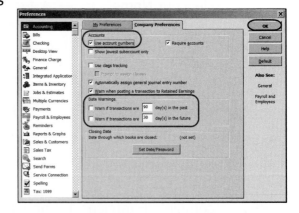

Step 7:   From the menu bar, select Edit; Preferences. Click on the My Preferences tab and select Checking. Put a check mark next to "Open the Write Check Form with…account," the "Open the

Pay Bills form with…account," and the "Open the make deposits form with…account." For each of these selections, choose the Home State Bank account.

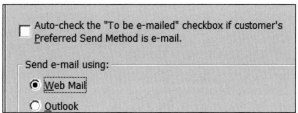

Click [OK] to save selections.

Step 8: From the menu bar, select Edit; Preferences. Click on My Preferences tab and select Send Forms. Uncheck box next to "Auto-check the To be e-mailed" checkbox if customer's Preferred Send Method is e-mail." In the e-mail using area, select Web Mail.

To save preferences, click [OK]. When the Warning window says that QuickBooks must close all its open windows to change this preference, click [OK].

Step 9: From the menu bar, select Edit; Preferences, Items & Inventory, Company Preferences tab. Put a check mark next to Inventory and purchase orders are active. Compare your Inventory & Items Preferences window to the one shown on the next page.

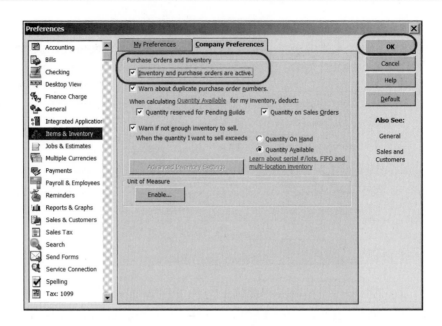

Click [**OK**] to save. Click [Home] to display the Home page.

CHART OF ACCOUNTS

Step 10: Delete the following accounts:

48300 Sales Discounts
51800 Merchant Account Fees
80000 Ask My Accountant

Step 11: Change the following accounts names and delete what currently displays as the Description. *Hint: Add account number 10000 to Home State Bank-Cash.*

Account	New Name	Type	Tax Line Mapping
Home State Bank	**Home State Bank-Cash**	**Bank**	**B/S-Assets: Cash**
Security Deposits Asset	**Prepaid Insurance**	**Other Current Asset**	**B/S-Assets: Other Current Assets**
Capital Stock	**Paid in Capital**	**Equity**	**B/S-Liabs/Eq.: Paid in or Capital Surplus**
Dividends Paid	**Dividends**	**Equity**	**Unassigned**

Opening Balance Equity	**Common Stock**	**Equity**	**B/S-Liabs/Eq.:** **Capital Stock** **Common Stock**
Utilities	**Utilities Expense**	**Expense**	**Other Deductions:** **Utilities**

Step 12: Add Account No. 26000.

New Account	**Description**	**Type**	**Income Tax Line**
Your Name Notes Payable	**Loans from stockholders**	**Long Term Liability**	**B/S-Liabs/Eq.:** **Loans from stockholders**

Step 13: You purchased Your Name Hardware Store in December of last year. (*HINT:* Use 12/31/last year to enter opening balances.) Use this Balance Sheet to record the beginning balances. Then go to the Report Center and display your Account Listing to confirm that your work so far is correct.

Your Name Hardware Store Balance Sheet January 1, 20XX (Your current year)		
ASSETS		
Current Assets		
Home State Bank-Cash	$ 80,000.00	
Prepaid Insurance	2,900.00	
Total Current Assets		$82,900.00
Fixed Assets		
Furniture and Equipment	6,000.00	
Total Fixed Assets		6,000.00
Total Assets		$88,900.00
LIABILITIES AND STOCKHOLDERS' EQUITY		
Your Name Notes Payable	9,500.00	
Total Liabilities		$9,500.00
Common Stock		79,400.00
Total Liabilities and Equity		$88,900.00

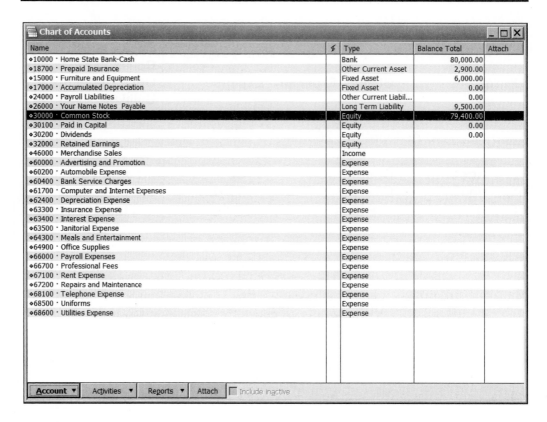

BACKUP

Step 14:   Make a backup to your USB drive. Use **Your Name Hardware Store Beginning Balances (Portable).QBM**. (*Hint:* Backups in Project 1 are portable files: File; Create Copy.) *Hint:* You may want to display the 12/31 balance sheet and compare to the one shown on the previous page.

VENDORS

Step 15:   Go to the Vendor Center and add the following vendors.

Vendor name:	AAA Shovels
Opening Balance.	0.00
As of:	1/1/current year
Company Name:	AAA Shovels
First Name:	Tim
Last Name:	Newton

Address:	**3000 First Avenue**
	Santa Cruz, CA 90036
Phone:	**310-555-2243**
FAX:	**310-555-2245**
E-mail:	**tim@aaa.biz**
Type:	**Suppliers**
Terms:	**Net 30**
Credit limit:	**15,000.00**

Vendor name:	**BBB Wheel barrows**
Opening Balance:	**0.00**
As of:	**1/1/current year**
Company Name:	**BBB Wheel barrows**
First Name:	**Baker**
Last Name:	**Bayou**
Business address:	**46011 Mesquite Street**
	El Paso, TX 76315
Phone:	**915-555-3000**
FAX:	**915-555-3100**
E-mail:	**Baker@BBB.com**
Type:	**Suppliers**
Terms:	**Net 30**
Credit limit:	**15,000.00**

Vendor name:	**CCC Wagons**
Opening Balance:	**0.00**
As of:	**1/1/current year**
Company Name:	**CCC Wagons**
First Name:	**Caitlin**
Last Name:	**Conner**
Address:	**2301 Dirt Road**
	Dugout, AZ 86003
Phone:	**928-555-2288**
FAX:	**928-555-2299**
E-mail:	**Caitlin@CCC.net**
Type:	**Suppliers**
Terms:	**Net 30**
Credit limit:	**15,000.00**

INVENTORY ITEMS

Step 16: Enter the following inventory parts:

Item name/number:	**Shovels**
Purchase description:	**Shovels**
Purchase cost:	**15.00**
COGS account:	50000, Cost of Goods Sold
Preferred vendor:	AAA Shovels
Sales description:	**Shovels**
Sales price:	**30.00**
Income account:	46000, Merchandise Sales
Inventory account:	12100, Inventory Asset
On hand:	0.00
Total value:	0.00
As of:	01/01/20XX

Item name/number:	**Wheel barrows**
Purchase description:	**Wheel barrows**
Purchase cost:	**75.00**
COGS account:	50000, Cost of Goods Sold
Preferred vendor:	BBB Wheel barrows
Sales description:	**Wheel barrows**
Sales price:	**100.00**
Income account:	46000, Merchandise Sales
Inventory account:	12100,Inventory Asset
On hand:	0.00
Total value:	0.00
As of:	01/01/20XX

Item name/number:	**Wagons**
Purchase description:	**Wagons**
Purchase cost:	**20.00**
COGS account:	Cost of Goods Sold
Preferred vendor:	CCC Wagons
Sales description:	Wagons
Sales price:	**50.00**
Income account:	Merchandise Sales
Inventory account:	Inventory Asset
On hand:	0.00
Total value:	0.00
As of:	01/01/20XX

CUSTOMERS

Step 17: Go to the Customer Center and add the following retail
          Customers:

Customer name:	**Dawn Bright**
Opening Balance:	**0.00**
As of:	**1/1/20XX**
First Name:	**Dawn**
Last Name:	**Bright**
Bill/Ship address:	**1800 W. Peoria Avenue**
	Reno, NV 92731
Phone:	**503-555-8630**
E-mail:	**db@myemail.com**
Type:	**Retail**
Terms:	Net 30
Credit limit:	**10,000.00**
Preferred payment method:	Check

Customer name:	**Roy Lars**
Opening Balance:	**0.00**
As of:	**1/2/20XX**
First Name:	**Roy**
Last Name:	**Lars**
Bill/Ship address:	**603 Nature Drive**
	Reno, NV 97401
Phone:	**541-555-7845**
E-mail:	**roy@mail.biz**
Type:	Retail
Terms:	Net 30
Credit limit:	**10,000.00**
Preferred payment method:	Check

Customer name:	**Shar Watsonville**
Opening Balance:	**0.00**
As of:	**1/1/20XX**
First Name:	**Shar**
Last Name:	**Watsonville**
Bill/Ship address:	**3455 West 20th Avenue**
	Reno, NV 97402
Phone:	**541-555-9233**

E-mail:	**sharon@email.com**
Type:	**Retail**
Terms:	Net 30
Credit limit:	**10,000.00**
Preferred payment method:	Check

Customer name:	**Credit Card Sales**
Opening Balance:	**0.00**
As of:	**1/1/20XX**
Type:	**Retail**

BACKUP

Step 18: Make a backup to your USB drive. Use **Your Name Hardware Store Vendors Inventory Customers (Portable).QBM** as the filename.

TRANSACTIONS FROM SOURCE DOCUMENT ANALYSIS

Step 19: After analyzing the source documents, record the appropriate transactions. All transactions occur during January of your current year.

AAA SHOVELS
INVOICE

BILL TO	Your Name Hardware Store Your address Reno, NV 89557	SHIP TO	Your Name Hardware Store Your address Reno, NV 89557	Invoice # 74A
				Invoice Date January 6
				Customer ID

| DATE | YOUR ORDER # | OUR ORDER # | SALES REP. | F.O.B. | SHIP VIA | TERMS | TAX ID |
| | | | | | | | |

QTY	ITEM	UNITS	DESCRIPTION	DISCOUNT %	TAXABLE	UNIT PRICE	TOTAL
25			shovels			15.00	375.00
						Subtotal	375.00
						Tax	
						Shipping	
						Miscellaneous	
						BALANCE DUE	375.00

CCC WAGONS
INVOICE

BILL TO	SHIP TO	
Your Name Hardware Store You're address Reno, NV 89557	Your Name Hardware Store Your address Reno, NV 89557	Invoice # 801 Invoice Date January 6 Customer ID

DATE	YOUR ORDER #	OUR ORDER #	SALES REP.	F.O.B.	SHIP VIA	TERMS	TAX ID

QTY	ITEM	UNITS	DESCRIPTION	DISCOUNT %	TAXABLE	UNIT PRICE	TOTAL
30			Wagons			20.00	600.00
						Subtotal	600.00
						Tax	
						Shipping	
						Miscellaneous	
						BALANCE DUE	600.00

BBB
WHEEL BARROWS
INVOICE

BILL TO	SHIP TO	
Your Name Hardware Store Your address Reno, NV 89557	Your Name Hardware Store Your address Reno, NV 89557	Invoice # ER555 Invoice Date January 6 Customer ID

DATE	YOUR ORDER #	OUR ORDER #	SALES REP.	F.O.B.	SHIP VIA	TERMS	TAX ID

QTY	ITEM	UNITS	DESCRIPTION	DISCOUNT %	TAXABLE	UNIT PRICE	TOTAL
32			Wheel barrows			75.00	2,400.00
						Subtotal	2,400.00
						Tax	
						Shipping	
						Miscellaneous	
						BALANCE DUE	2,400.00

Your Name Hardware Store			SALES RECEIPT	

Your Address
Reno, NV 89557   Your phone number

SOLD TO:
Credit card sales

SALES NUMBER 1
SALES DATE January 10

SHIPPED TO:

QUANTITY	DESCRIPTION		UNIT PRICE	AMOUNT
4	Shovels			120.00
5	Wheel barrows			500.00
8	Wagons			400.00
			SUBTOTAL	1,020.00
			TAX	
			FREIGHT	
				$1,020.00

DIRECT ALL INQUIRIES TO:
Your Name   Your Name Hardware Store
Your phone number   Your Address
email: your email   Reno, NV 89557

THANK YOU FOR YOUR BUSINESS!

Your Name Hardware Store			SALES RECEIPT	

Your Address
Reno, NV 89557   Your phone number

SOLD TO:
Credit card sales

SALES NUMBER 2
SALES DATE January 12

SHIPPED TO:

QUANTITY	DESCRIPTION		UNIT PRICE	AMOUNT
3	Shovels			90.00
4	Wheel barrows			400.00
5	Wagons			250.00
			SUBTOTAL	740.00
			TAX	
			FREIGHT	
				$740.00

DIRECT ALL INQUIRIES TO:
Your Name   Your Name Hardware Store
Your phone number   Your Address
email: your email   Reno, NV 89557

THANK YOU FOR YOUR BUSINESS!

Your Name Hardware Store — INVOICE

Your Address
Reno, NV 89557   Your phone number

SOLD TO:
Dawn Bright   INVOICE NUMBER | 1
1800 W. Peoria Avenue   INVOICE DATE | January 12
Reno, NV 92731

SHIPPED TO:
Same

QUANTITY	DESCRIPTION	UNIT PRICE	AMOUNT
1	Shovel		30.00
		SUBTOTAL	30.00
		TAX	
		FREIGHT	
			$30.00

DIRECT ALL INQUIRIES TO: **MAKE ALL CHECKS PAYABLE TO:**   PAY THIS
Your Name   Your Name Hardware Store   AMOUNT
Your phone number   Attn: Accounts Receivable
email: your email   Your Address
                                     Reno, NV 89557

THANK YOU FOR YOUR BUSINESS!

Your Name Hardware Store — SALES RECEIPT

Your Address
Reno, NV 89557   Your phone number

SOLD TO:
Credit card sales   SALES NUMBER | 3
                                                 SALES DATE | January 17

SHIPPED TO:

QUANTITY	DESCRIPTION	UNIT PRICE	AMOUNT
2	Shovels		60.00
7	Wheel barrows		700.00
3	Wagons		150.00
		SUBTOTAL	910.00
		TAX	
		FREIGHT	
			$910.00

DIRECT ALL INQUIRIES TO:
Your Name   Your Name Hardware Store
Your phone number   Your Address
email: your email   Reno, NV 89557

THANK YOU FOR YOUR BUSINESS!

Memo

Date: 1/20 current year

Re: Vendor Payments

Your Name Hardware Store pays all outstanding vendor bills for a total of $3,375.00. (*Hint:* The required payment method is Check from Home State Bank; assign check numbers 1-3 automatically.) Refer to the remittances that follow.

AAA Shovels:	$375.00
BBB Wheel barrows	2,400.00
CCC Wagons	600.00
Total	$3,375.00

Note: On the Pay Bills window, select Assign check number. In the Check No. field, type **1, 2, 3**.

REMITTANCE

Invoice #	74A
Customer ID	Your Name Hardware Store
Date	January 20
Amount Enclosed	375.00

AAA Shovels
3000 First Avenue
Santa Cruz, CA
90036

PHONE (310)5552243
FAX (310)555-2245
E-MAIL tim@aaa.biz

REMITTANCE

Invoice #	ER555
Customer ID	Your Name Hardware Store
Date	January 20
Amount Enclosed	2,400.00

BBB Wheel barrows
46011 Mesquite St.
El Paso, TX 76315

PHONE (915)555-3000
FAX (915)555-3100
E-MAIL Baker@BBB.com

REMITTANCE

Invoice #	801
Customer ID	Your Name Hardware Store
Date	January 20
Amount Enclosed	600.00

CCC Wagons
2301 Dirt Road
Dugout, AZ 86003

PHONE   (928)555-2288
FAX   (928)555-2299
E-MAIL   Caitlin@CCC.net

Your Name Hardware Store   SALES RECEIPT

Your Address
Reno, NV 89557   Your phone number

SOLD TO:
Credit card sales

SALES NUMBER | 4
SALES DATE | January 21

SHIPPED TO:

QUANTITY	DESCRIPTION	UNIT PRICE	AMOUNT
6	Shovels		180.00
8	Wheel barrows		800.00
9	Wagons		450.00
		SUBTOTAL	1,430.00
		TAX	
		FREIGHT	
			$1,430.00

DIRECT ALL INQUIRIES TO:
Your Name   Your Name Hardware Store
Your phone number   Your Address
email: your email   Reno, NV 89557

THANK YOU FOR YOUR BUSINESS!

Memo

Date: 1/21 current year

Re: Rent

Write Check No. 4 to vendor, Stevens Rentals, for $1,350 in payment of rent. (*Hint:* Add vendor as needed; uncheck To be printed. Account: Rent Expense.)

Your Name Hardware Store   INVOICE

Your Address
Reno, NV 89557   Your phone number

SOLD TO:
Shar Watsonville   INVOICE NUMBER | 2
3455 West 20th Avenue   INVOICE DATE | January 22
Reno, NV 97402

SHIPPED TO:
Same

QUANTITY	DESCRIPTION	UNIT PRICE	AMOUNT
1	Wagon		50.00
		SUBTOTAL	50.00
		TAX	
		FREIGHT	

$50.00
PAY THIS
AMOUNT

DIRECT ALL INQUIRIES TO: **MAKE ALL CHECKS PAYABLE TO:**
Your Name   Your Name Hardware Store
Your phone number   Attn: Accounts Receivable
email: your email   Your Address
                                       Reno, NV 89557

THANK YOU FOR YOUR BUSINESS!

AAA SHOVELS
INVOICE

BILL TO
Your Name Hardware Store
Your address
Reno, NV 89557

SHIP TO
Your Name Hardware Store
Your address
Reno, NV 89557

Invoice # 88A
Invoice Date   January 24
Customer ID

DATE	YOUR ORDER #	OUR ORDER #	SALES REP.	F.O.B.	SHIP VIA	TERMS	TAX ID

QTY	ITEM	UNITS	DESCRIPTION	DISCOUNT %	TAXABLE	UNIT PRICE	TOTAL
15			shovels			15.00	225.00
						Subtotal	225.00
						Tax	
						Shipping	
						Miscellaneous	
						BALANCE DUE	225.00

CCC WAGONS
INVOICE

BILL TO	Your Name Hardware Store Your address Reno, NV 89557	SHIP TO	Your Name Hardware Store Your address Reno, NV 89557	Invoice # 962
				Invoice Date January 24
				Customer ID

DATE	YOUR ORDER #	OUR ORDER #	SALES REP.	F.O.B.	SHIP VIA	TERMS	TAX ID

QTY	ITEM	UNITS	DESCRIPTION	DISCOUNT %	TAXABLE	UNIT PRICE	TOTAL
18			Wagons			20.00	360.00
						Subtotal	360.00
						Tax	
						Shipping	
						Miscellaneous	
						BALANCE DUE	360.00

BBB
WHEEL BARROWS
INVOICE

BILL TO	Your Name Hardware Store Your address Reno, NV 89557	SHIP TO	Your Name Hardware Store Your address Reno, NV 89557	Invoice # ER702
				Invoice Date January 24
				Customer ID

DATE	YOUR ORDER #	OUR ORDER #	SALES REP.	F.O.B.	SHIP VIA	TERMS	TAX ID

QTY	ITEM	UNITS	DESCRIPTION	DISCOUNT %	TAXABLE	UNIT PRICE	TOTAL
20			Wheel barrows			75.00	1,500.00
						Subtotal	1,500.00
						Tax	
						Shipping	
						Miscellaneous	
						BALANCE DUE	1,500.00

Your Name Hardware Store   SALES RECEIPT

Your Address
Reno, NV 89557   Your phone number

SOLD TO:
Credit card sales   SALES NUMBER | 5
                                                     SALES DATE | January 26

SHIPPED TO:

QUANTITY	DESCRIPTION	UNIT PRICE	AMOUNT
6	Shovels		180.00
6	Wheel barrows		600.00
6	Wagons		300.00
		SUBTOTAL	1,080.00
		TAX	
		FREIGHT	
			$1,080.00

DIRECT ALL INQUIRIES TO:
Your Name   Your Name Hardware Store
Your phone number   Your Address
email: your email   Reno, NV 89557

THANK YOU FOR YOUR BUSINESS!

**Your Name
Hardware Store**

Memo

Date: 1/27 current year

Re: Your Name Notes Payable

Write Check No. 5 to Your Name (*HINT:* Add New, Other) for $420.80 in payment of Your Name Notes Payable. Use the following Expenses distribution:

Account	Debit	Credit
Your Name Notes Payable	340.00	
Interest Expense	80.80	
Home State Bank		420.80

Your Name Hardware Store

Memo

Date: 1/27 current year

Re: Utilities

Write Check No. 6 to Rainer Utilities for $225.65 in payment of electricity and gas expenses. (*Hint:* Add new vendor, Account Utilities Expense.)

Your Name Hardware Store   SALES RECEIPT

Your Address
Reno, NV 89557   Your phone number

SOLD TO:
Credit card sales

SALES NUMBER	6
SALES DATE	January 29

SHIPPED TO:

QUANTITY	DESCRIPTION	UNIT PRICE	AMOUNT
4	Shovels		120.00
5	Wheel barrows		500.00
8	Wagons		400.00
		SUBTOTAL	1,020.00
		TAX	
		FREIGHT	
			$1,020.00

DIRECT ALL INQUIRIES TO:
Your Name   Your Name Hardware Store
Your phone number   Your Address
email: your email   Reno, NV 89557

THANK YOU FOR YOUR BUSINESS!

Your Name Hardware Store

Memo

Date: 1/30 current year

Re: Customer payments

Received checks in full payment of customer accounts:

1. Received a check in full payment of Dawn Bright's account, $30.

2. Received a check in full payment of Shar Watsonville's account, $50.

Your Name Hardware Store

Memo

Date: 1/30 current year

Re: Credit Card Receipts

Record deposit to Home State Bank in the amount of $6,280 ($6,200 from credit card sales; $30 and $50 from customer sales.)

	Home State Bank				
	Your Name Hardware Store				
	Your Address	Checks:	Check Number	Amount	
	Reno, NV 89557	1	Credit cards	$ 6,200.00	
	Your phone number	2	D. Bright	$ 30.00	
		3	S. Watsonville	$ 50.00	
		4			
Date:	January 30	5			
		6			
List of Deposits:		7			
Coin:	**Totals:**	8			
Quarters:	$ -	9			
Dimes:	$ -	10			
Nickles:	$ -	11			
Pennies	$ -	12			
Total:	$ -	13			
Cash:	**Totals:**	14			
$1	$ -	15			
$5	$ -	16			
$10	$ -	17			
$20	$ -	18			
$50	$ -	19			
$100	$ -	20			
Total:	$ -		**Totals:**	$ 6,280.00	
Total Cash:	$ -		**Total Deposit:**	$ 6,280.00	

Below is a list of the transactions recorded during January:

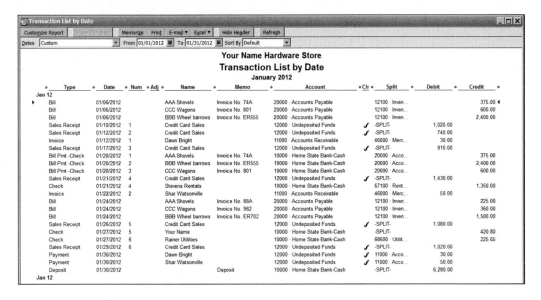

BACKUP

Step 20: Back up to your USB drive. The suggested filename is **Your Name Hardware Store January (Portable).QBM**.

BANK RECONCILIATION

Step 21: Complete account reconciliation for Account No. 10000, Home State Bank-Cash on 01/31/20XX. Use the bank statement shown here. (*HINT:* Remember to enter the $25.00 for Bank Service Charges.)

Statement of Account Home State Bank January 1 to January 31 Account No. 937522			Your Name Hardware Store Your Address Reno, NV	
REGULAR CHECKING				
Previous Balance	12/31	$80,000.00		
Deposits		6,280.00		
Checks (-)		5,371.45		
Service Charges (-)	1/31	25.00		
Ending Balance	1/31	**$80,883.55**		
DEPOSITS				
	1/30	30.00	Dawn Bright	
	1/30	50.00	Shar Watsonville	
		6,200.00	Credit Card	
CHECKS				
	1/20	375.00	1	
	1/20	2,400.00	2	
	1/20	600.00	3	
	1/21	1,350.00	4	
	1/27	420.80	5	
	1/28	225.65	6	

REPORTS

Step 22:   Print the Summary Reconciliation report.

Step 23:   Print the journal (all dates).

Step 24:   Print the trial balance (01/31/20XX).

Step 25:   Print the vendor balance detail; customer balance detail; and inventory stock status by item.

Step 26: Print the income and expense graph by account and expenses (01/01/20XX to 01/31/20XX).

Step 27: Print the January financial statements: Profit & Loss-Standard, Balance Sheet-Standard, and Statement of Cash Flow.

Step 28: Print the audit trail (all dates).

BACKUP AND E-MAIL

Step 29: Make a backup of Project 1, Your Name Hardware Store to your USB drive. Use **Your Name Hardware Store Complete (Portable).QBM** as the file name.

Step 30: Send an e-mail message to your professor and to yourself with the Your Name Hardware Store Complete (Portable) file attached. Type **Your Name Hardware Store Complete** in the Subject line of the e-mail.

If PDF files are the preferred format for saving reports, email your instructor.

Step 31: Receive the Your Name Hardware Store Complete e-mail with the correct company file attached. Print it.

Step 32: Turn in completed Check Your Progress: Project 1 and required printouts to your professor.

Student Name_____**Date**_____

CHECK YOUR PROGRESS: PROJECT 1, Your Name Hardware Store

1. What are the total debit and credit balances on the Trial Balance? _____

2. What are the total assets on January 31? _____

3. What is the balance in the Home State Bank account on January 31? _____

4. How much is total income on January 31? _____

5. How much net income (net loss) is reported on January 31? _____

6. What is the balance in the Inventory-Shovels account on January 31? _____

7. What is the balance in the Inventory-Wheel barrows account on January 31? _____

8. What is the balance in the Inventory-Wagons account on January 31? _____

9. During January sales per week for shovels were? _____

10. What is the balance in the Common Stock account on January 31? _____

11. What is the total cost of goods sold on January 31? _____

12. Were any Accounts Payable incurred during the month of January? (Circle your answer.)   YES   NO

Project 2
Student-Designed Merchandising Business

You have learned how to complete the accounting cycle for merchandising businesses. Project 2 gives you a chance to create a merchandising business of your own.

You select retail as the business type, edit your business's Chart of Accounts, create beginning balances and transactions, and complete QuickBooks' computer accounting cycle. Project 2 also gives you an opportunity to review the software features learned so far.

Before you begin, you should design your business. You will need the following:

1. Company information that includes business name, address, and telephone number.

2. Select retail as the business type.

3. A Chart of Accounts

4. A beginning Balance Sheet for your business.

5. One month's transactions for your business. These transactions must include accounts receivable, accounts payable, inventory, sales, and dividends. You should have a minimum of 25 transactions; a maximum of 35 transactions. These transactions should result in a net income.

6. Complete another month of transactions that result in a net loss.

A suggested checklist of printouts is shown on the next page.

PROJECT 2	
CHECKLIST OF PRINTOUTS	
Ask your professor how these should be turned in…	
	Chart of Accounts
	Check Register
	Vendor List
	Item List
	Customer List
	Reconciliation-Summary and Detail
	Journal
	Trial Balance
	Profit & Loss-Standard
	Balance Sheet-Standard
	Statement of Cash Flows
	Audit Trail

Appendix A
Review of Accounting Principles

Appendix A is a review of basic accounting principles and procedures. Standard accounting procedures are based on the double-entry system. This means that each business transaction is expressed with one or more debits and one or more credits in a journal entry and then posted to the ledger. The debits in each transaction must equal the credits.

The double-entry accounting system is based on the following premise: each account has two sides—a debit (left) side and credit (right) side. This is stated in the *accounting equation* as:

Assets = Liabilities + Equities

Assets are the organization's resources that have a future or potential value. Asset accounts include: Cash, Marketable Securities, Accounts Receivable, Supplies, Prepaids, Inventory, Investments, Equipment, Land, Buildings, etc.

Liabilities are the organization's responsibilities to others. Liability accounts include: Accounts Payable, Notes Payable, Unearned Rent, etc.

Equities are the difference between the organization's assets and liabilities. Equity accounts for organizations that are sole proprietorships or partnerships include: Capital and Withdrawals. Equity accounts for organizations that are corporations include contributed capital accounts like Common Stock which represent external ownership and Retained Earnings which represent internal ownership interests. Temporary equity-related accounts known as revenue and expense accounts recognize an organization's income producing activities and the related costs consumed or expired during the period.

Since assets are on the left side of the accounting equation, the left side of the account increases. This is the usual balance, too; assets increase on the left side and have a debit balance. Liabilities and Equities accounts are on the right side of the equation. Therefore, they increase on the right side and normally carry credit balances.

The McGraw-Hill Companies, Inc., *Computer Accounting Essentials with QuickBooks 2012*

Another way to show the accounting equation and double-entry is illustrated below.

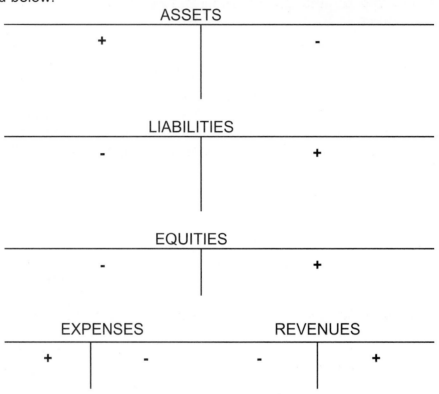

Each element of the accounting equation, Assets, Liabilities, and Equities, behaves similarly to their placement in the equation. Assets have debit balances; Liabilities have credit balances; Equities have credit balances; Expenses have debit balances because they decrease equity; and Revenues have credit balances because they increase equity.

In computerized accounting it is important to number each account according to a system. This is called the Chart of Accounts. The Chart of Accounts is a listing of all the general ledger accounts. The QuickBooks chart of accounts shows the account number and name, Type (this classifies the accounts for financial statements) and Balance total. To view the chart of accounts: go to the QuickBooks Home page Company pane and click on the Chart of Accounts icon. The Your Name Retailers Inc. chart of account is shown on the next page as an example of a typical merchandising business' chart of accounts.

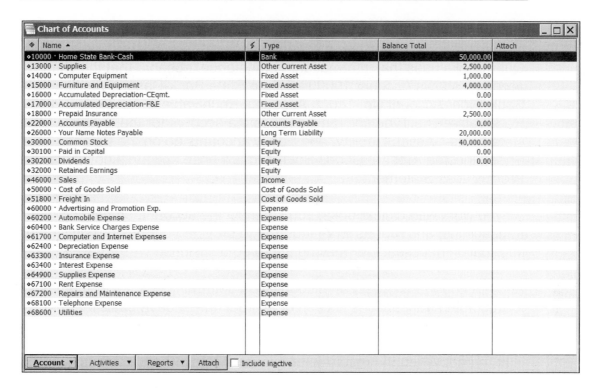

Report information in the form of financial statements is important to accounting. The Balance Sheet reports the financial position of the business on a specific date. It shows that assets are equal to liabilities plus equities—the accounting equation. The Profit & Loss shows the difference between revenue and expenses for a specified period of time (month, quarter, or year). The Income Statement is another name for Profit & Loss. QuickBooks tracks revenue and expense data for an entire year. At the end of the year when all revenue and expense accounts are closed, the resulting net income or loss is moved into the equity account, Retained Earnings. The Statement of Cash Flows reports the operating, financial, and investing activities for the period. It shows the sources of cash coming into the business and the destination of the cash going out.

The most important task you have is accurately recording transactions into the appropriate accounts. QuickBooks helps you by organizing the software into Home, Vendors, Customers, Employees Company, Banking, and Report Centers. By selecting the appropriate Center and/or icon, you can record transactions into the right place using easy-to-complete forms. Once transactions are entered, QuickBooks keeps this information in a database. Then the data can be accessed and viewed as journal entries or transaction listings, account or ledger activities, reports, or analysis.

One of the most important tasks is deciding how to enter transactions. Recording and categorizing business transactions will determine how QuickBooks uses that information. For instance, observe that the chart of accounts shows Account 10000 – Home State Bank-Cash, classified as a Bank Type; Account No. 11000 Accounts Receivable is Accounts Receivable. The Type column classifies the account for the financial statements—Asset, Liability, and Equity accounts go on the Balance Sheet; Income, Cost of Goods Sold, and Expense accounts go on the Profit & Loss Statement.

As you work with QuickBooks, you see how the accounts, recording of transactions, and reports work together to provide your business with the information necessary for making informed decisions.

Another important aspect of accounting is determining whether the basis for recording transactions is cash or accrual. In the cash basis method, revenues and expenses are recognized when cash changes hands. In other words, when the customer pays for their purchase, the transaction is recorded. When the resource or expense is paid for by the business, the transaction is recorded.

In the accrual method of accounting, revenues and expenses are recognized when they occur. In other words, if the company purchases inventory on April 1, the transaction is recorded on April 1. If inventory is sold on account on April 15, the transaction is done on April 15 *not* when cash is received from customers. Accrual basis accounting is seen as more accurate because assets, liabilities, revenues, and expenses are recorded when they actually happen.

The chart on the next page summarizes Appendix A, Review of Accounting Principles.

ACCOUNTING EQUATION:	Assets =	Liabilities +	Owners Equities +	Revenues –	Expenses
Definition:	Something that has future or potential value "Resources"	Responsibilities to others "Payables" "Unearned"	Internal and External ownership	Recognition of value creation	Expired, used, or consumed costs or resources
Debit Rules: DR	Increase	Decrease	Decrease	Decrease	Increase
Credit Rules:CR	Decrease	Increase	Increase	Increase	Decrease
Account Types and Examples	**Current Assets:** Cash, Marketable Securities, Accounts Receivable, Inventory, Prepaids **Plant Assets:** Land, Buildings, Equipment, Accumulated Depreciation **Noncurrent Assets:** Investments, Intangibles	**Current Liabilities:** Accounts Payable, Unearned Revenue, Advances from Customer **Noncurrent or Long-term Liabilities:** Bonds Payable, Notes Payables, Mortgage Payable	**Sole Proprietor:** (both internal and external) Name, Capital; Name, Withdrawals **Partnership:** (both internal and external) Partner A, Capital; Partner A, Withdrawals, etc. **Corporation:** External: Common Stock, Preferred Stock, Paid-in Capital Internal: Retained Earnings, Dividends	**Operating Revenue:** Sales, Fees Earned, Rent Income, Contract Revenue **Other Revenue:** Interest Income	**Product/Services Expenses:** Cost of Goods Sold, Cost of Sales **Operating Expenses:** Selling Expenses, Administrative Expense, General Expense, Salary Expense, Rent Expense, Depreciation Expense, Insurance Expense **Other Expenses:** Interest Expense

T-Account Rules

Assets		Liabilities		Owners Equities		Revenues		Expenses	
Acquire resources	Consume resources	Pay bills Recognize earnings	Buy on credit Receive cash or other assets before earning it	Internal: Net Loss External: Owners reduce ownership thru withdrawals or dividends	Internal: Net Income External: Investment made by owners in company	Sales returns Sales discount given	Sales Earned Income		Resources consumed expired or used
increase	*decrease*	*decrease*	*increase*	*decrease*	*increase*	*decrease*	*increase*		*Increase* *decrease*

The McGraw-Hill Companies, Inc., *Computer Accounting Essentials with QuickBooks 2012*

Basic Financial Statements:

Income Statement
Revenue-Expense=Net Income (NI) or
Net Loss (NL)
(Prepare first)

Statement of Equity
Beginning* + NI (or –NL) - (Dividends or Withdrawals) = Ending*
*for Sole Proprietors and Partnerships use "Capital" and Withdrawals
for Corporations use "Retained Earnings" and Dividends
(Prepare second)

Balance Sheet
Assets=Liabilities + Equities
(Prepare third)

Statement of Cash Flows
Operating+/-Investing+/-Financing+Beginning Cash=Ending Cash
(Prepare last)

QUICKBOOKS FOR THE MAC

To learn about Windows operating system compatibility with the Mac, go online to http://www.apple.com/macosx/compatibility/.

Setup is simple and safe for your Mac files. After you've completed the installation, you can boot up your Mac using either Mac OS X or Windows. Or, if you want to run Windows and Mac applications at the same time, without rebooting, you can install Windows using VMware or Parallels software. VMware and Parallels software are sold separately.

QuickBooks also has a Macintosh version. To learn more, go online to http://proadvisor.intuit.com/product/accounting-software/pro-mac-financial-management-software.jsp.

The 140-day software CD included with *Computer Accounting Essentials with QuickBooks 2012* is PC compatible (Windows XP, Vista and 7).

INSTALLATION AND REGISTRATION

There is one CD included with the text, QuickBooks 2012 Student Trial Edition software. This is a 140-day single user copy of the software.

Follow these steps to install software and register the software.

1. Close all programs and disable anti-virus software.
2. Insert the QuickBooks 2012 Student Trial Edition CD in your CD drive.
3. Follow the screen prompts to install the software.
4. Use the License and Product number located on the QuickBooks software CD envelope.
5. You can use the software for 30 days without registering. There are three ways to register:

    a. Register the software during installation.

    b. From the menu bar select, Help; Register QuickBooks.
        (If Register QuickBooks is <u>not</u> shown on the Help menu, QuickBooks has been registered.)

c. Register QuickBooks by calling 888-246-8848 or 800-316-1068; outside US, 520-901-3220.)

SOFTWARE REGISTRATION

If Register QuickBooks is shown on the Help menu, you have not registered your copy of QuickBooks. When QuickBooks is open, you can verify that your copy of QuickBooks is registered by pressing the <F2> function key. The Product Information window appears and displays either REGISTERED or UNREGISTERED based on the registration status. Once the software included with the textbook is registered, you have access for 140 days.

QUICKBOOKS FOR THE CLASSROOM

For software installation in the school's computer lab or classroom, please refer to the Intuit Education Program online at www.Intuitaccountants.com/educationyacht.

As of this writing, the cost for classroom site licenses is:

- 10 computers, $300.00*
- 25 computers, $460.00
- 50 computers, $690.00
*Pricing is subject to change.

These site licenses do not allow Multi-User Access. Multi-user mode means more than one person (up to five) work with a single company data file at the same time. QuickBooks site licenses do not have this feature.

To order a classroom site license, call the Intuit Education Program, 1-866-570-3843, or email education@intuit.com.

UPDATE QUICKBOOKS

When you start QuickBooks, if this window appears, you may want to update the software. Check with your instructor for his or her preference. As of this writing Release 4 (R4) is the update available.

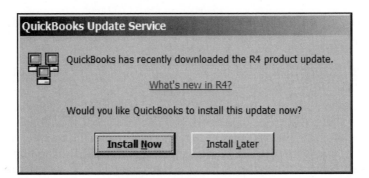

SET UP AN EXTERNAL ACCOUNTANT USER

If a Set Up an External Accountant User appears when you start QB, or open a company, put a check mark in the Don't show this again box, then click **No**.

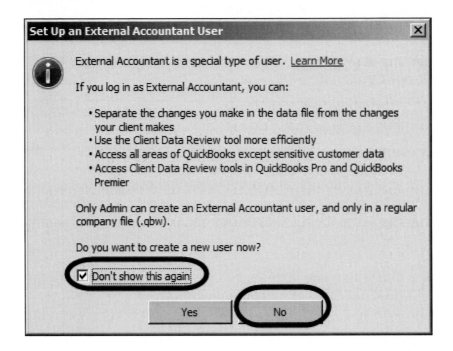

DEFAULT FILE LOCATIONS

Company Files

The default location for company files with qbw extensions is:

Windows Vista\Windows 7: C:\Users\Public\Public Documents\Intuit\ QuickBooks\Company Files

Windows XP: C:\Documents and Settings\All Users\Documents\Intuit\ QuickBooks\Company Files

Recommended Backup Routine: .QBB and .QBM Extensions

Back up your company file at the end of each classroom session or each day to a network drive; external hard drive; removable storage device such as a CD, USB flash drive, or to a remote site over the Internet.

Do not store routine backups on your computer's hard drive where you store your working data—if your computer's hard disk fails, you may lose your backup files as well as your working data.

Set Default Location for Backups

When you first use the backup wizard, you need to enter the default location where you want to store your backups. You can set or change this default using these instructions.

1. Go to the File menu and click Create Copy or Create Backup to start the backup wizard.

2. Click Backup Copy, click <Next>, and then click the Options button.

3. Click Browse to locate the location where you want to store your backups. The directory you choose remains your default until you change it.

Backups can be made to external media, a hard drive location, or network drive location. The textbook recommends a USB flash drive.

SET UP FOLDERS FOR DATA MANAGEMENT

You may want to organize QuickBooks file types in separate folders. QuickBooks file types include portable backup files (.QBM extensions) and company files (.QBW extensions).

How Do I Show File Extensions?

To show files extensions, follow these steps.

1. Right-click on the <Start> button; left-click Explore. (The selection in Windows 7 is Open Windows Explorer.)

2. Click on the Organize down-arrow. Select Folder and Search Options. Click on the View tab.

3. Uncheck Hide extensions for known file types.

☐ Hide extensions for known file types

4. Click <OK> to close the Folder Options window.

5. Close Windows Explorer.

QuickBooks Company Files Folder

You may want to set up a folder for QuickBooks company files. QuickBooks company files end in the extension .QBW.
Before restoring files, set up a folder labeled QuickBooks Company Files_QBW.

QuickBooks Company Files_QBW
File folder

When you restore files in QuickBooks, a Save Company File as window appears. In the Save in field, select the QuickBooks Company Files_QBW folder.

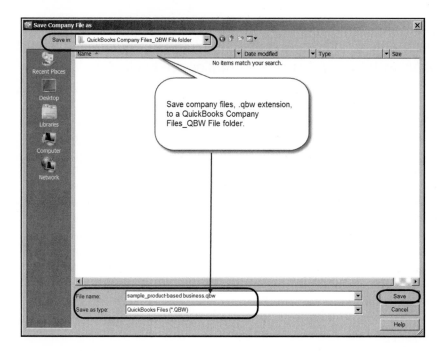

By saving company files to their own folder, you store the company files (.QBW extensions) in a different location than the backup files (.QBM extensions).

When a company is opened in QuickBooks, the following file extensions are associated with that company file:

1. .QBW: QuickBooks working file or company file
2. .DSN: Database source name
3. .ND: network data
4. .TLG: transaction logs
5. .LGB: little green box file contains encrypted information; for example, user names and passwords.

Your Name QB Backups Folder

After completing work, you are instructed to save the backed up files to a separate folder labeled Your Name QB Backups [use your first and last name].

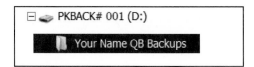

If all the chapters and projects are completed in *Computer Accounting Essentials with QuickBooks 2012,* 24 files are backed up.

sample_product-based business (Portable).QBM	QuickBooks Portable Company File	1,616 KB
Your Name Chapter 2 End (Portable).QBM	QuickBooks Portable Company File	1,619 KB
Your Name Chapter 3 October 1.QBB	QuickBooks Company Backup File	6,064 KB
Your Name Chapter 3 October Check Register (Backup Jan 04,2012 02...	QuickBooks Company Backup File	6,128 KB
Your Name Chapter 3 October End (Backup Jan 04,2012 03 03 PM).QBB	QuickBooks Company Backup File	6,196 KB
Your Name Chapter 4 End.QBB	QuickBooks Company Backup File	6,592 KB
Your Name Chapter 4 November.QBB	QuickBooks Company Backup File	6,480 KB
Your Name Chapter 4 Vendors and Inventory.QBB	QuickBooks Company Backup File	6,268 KB
Your Name Chapter 4 Vendors.QBB	QuickBooks Company Backup File	6,332 KB
Your Name Chapter 5 December Financial Statements.QBB	QuickBooks Company Backup File	6,816 KB
Your Name Chapter 5 December UTB.QBB	QuickBooks Company Backup File	6,808 KB
Your Name Chapter 5 EOY (Portable).QBM	QuickBooks Portable Company File	643 KB
Your Name Chapter 6 January Check Register.QBB	QuickBooks Company Backup File	6,880 KB
Your Name Chapter 6 January Financial Statements.QBB	QuickBooks Company Backup File	7,052 KB
Your Name Chapter 6 UTB.QBB	QuickBooks Company Backup File	6,980 KB
Your Name Exercise 4-2 December.QBB	QuickBooks Company Backup File	6,724 KB
Your Name Exercise 6-1 (Portable).QBM	QuickBooks Portable Company File	743 KB
Your Name Hardware Store (Backup Dec 14,2011 03 02 PM).QBB	QuickBooks Company Backup File	6,400 KB
Your Name Hardware Store Beginning Balances (Portable).QBM	QuickBooks Portable Company File	337 KB
Your Name Hardware Store Complete (Portable).QBM	QuickBooks Portable Company File	441 KB
Your Name Hardware Store January (Portable).QBM	QuickBooks Portable Company File	353 KB
Your Name Hardware Store Vendors Inventory Customers (Portable).QBM	QuickBooks Portable Company File	343 KB
Your Name Retailers Inc. (Backup Dec 14,2011 02 52 PM).QBB	QuickBooks Company Backup File	5,952 KB
Your Name sample_service-based business (Portable).QBM	QuickBooks Portable Company File	1,100 KB

Types of Backup Files

QuickBooks includes three types of backup files:

1. Backup copy (.QBB extensions)
2. Portable company file (.QBM extensions)
3. Accountant's copy (.QBX or .QBA extensions)

In *Computer Accounting Essentials with QuickBooks 2012*, the methods shown for backing up are the Portable company file (.QBM) selection or the Backup copy (.QBB) file. Portable company files are smaller than Backup copy files. For emailing a file, portable company files (.QBM) are recommended.

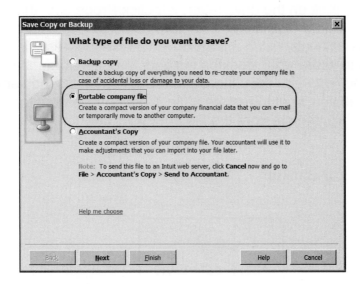

Backup Location No Longer Available

QuickBooks saves the location where files are backed up. If you decide to use another backup location, this Warning window will appear.

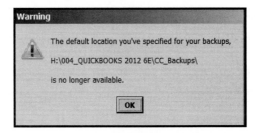

Click ![OK], then select the location where you want to back up. Type the file, then save.

Restore Previous Local Backup

If you want to restore a file previously backed up with the company that is currently open, used the File; Restore Previous Local Backup selection. The most recent file backed up is shown first on the list of backup files.

TROUBLESHOOTING BACKUP AND RESTORE: USING USB DRIVES

USB drives use different files systems. To see your USB drive's file system, right-click on the drive letter, left-click Properties, then select the General tab. Some USB drives are more reliable than others. If you are experiencing difficulty using a USB drive when either restoring from or backing up to it, use your Desktop instead. In other words, backup to your desktop first, then copy the file to a USB drive. Do the same thing in reverse when you want to restore a file. Copy the file from the USB drive to your desktop, then restore the file from your desktop instead of from a USB drive.

Create Copy or Backup

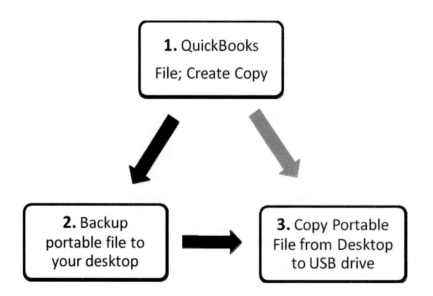

Restore a file

1. If the backup file resides on a USB drive, copy the file from the USB drive to your desktop.

2. Start QuickBooks. Open or restore the file from your desktop instead of the USB drive.

QBW File Already Exists

When restoring a file, if a screen prompts "[File name]…qbw already exists. Do you want to replace it?"

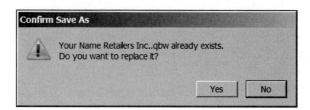

Click No . In the File name field, change the name slightly; for example, add your initials.

Now that you changed the file name, you can click Save to continue restoring your file. (*Hint:* Your Name Retailers Inc. is used in this example. Your file name may differ.)

You could also delete the files associated with the company. Then, restore the file without changing its name. The files associated with company files (.qbw extensions) are shown earlier in this appendix.

QuickBooks Login Password

When opening a QB company, if a QuickBooks Login window appears, click OK to continue. (*Hint:* You do not need to type a password if a password has <u>not</u> been set up.)

Or, if you set up a password, type it. In Chapter 2, the authors suggest that you do <u>not</u> type a password to avoid the need for typing one when restoring or opening company files.

QUICKBOOKS SUPPORT FROM INTUIT

QuickBooks support is available from Intuit, the publisher of QuickBooks software, at http://support.quickbooks.intuit.com/support.

From the support website, you can:

- Update your product.
- Get install help.
- Contact support.
- Type search words or error message number.

HELP WINDOWS

Use the <F1> function key for Help from any QuickBooks window. When you press <F1>, a Have a Question window appears. In the example below, <F1> was selected from the Home page.

You can search help or use the Live Community to find answers.

When the Chart of Accounts is selected, then <F1>, context-sensitive help appears.

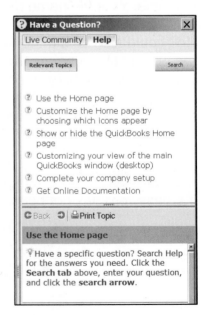

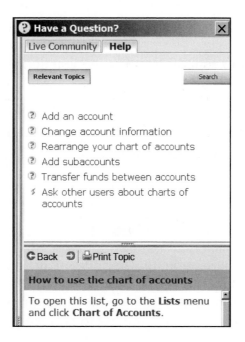

USE EXCEL WITH QUICKBOOKS

Your instructor may want you to email QuickBooks assignments completed in *Computer Accounting Essentials with QuickBooks 2012*. QuickBooks includes a way to export reports to Excel.

Follow these steps to export a QuickBooks report to Excel.

1. Display the report for the appropriate date.
2. You have two choices: E-mail, then select Send report as Excel; *or,* selecting the Excel button. In these steps you click Excel ▼ , Create New Worksheet. The Send Report to Excel window appears. Accept the default, in new workbook.
3. Click Export .
4. Excel opens. Save the workbook.
5. Close the QuickBooks report.

SAVE REPORT AS A PDF FILE

You can email reports as PDF files. When you send a report as a PDF file, the report is attached to an email message. If you do not have Acrobat Reader, you can download it for free from www.adobe.com.

1. Display the report you want to email as a PDF file.
2. Click E-mail, Send report as PDF.

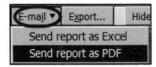

3. When the Email Security window appears, read the information. Then put a check mark in the Do not display this message in the future box. Click <OK>.
4. If a Sending E-mail using Outlook message appears, read it, then click <Close>. If a screens prompts to choose your e-mail method, do that.
5. Your email account opens. The report is an attached PDF file. Type the recipient's email address and send. Go to the File menu, and then click Save as PDF.

PRINTING REPORTS

There are numerous ways to print or display reports. For example, you can filter reports for the type of transaction.

After completing an Exercise, let's say you want to look at the vendor bills paid.

1. From the menu bar, select Reports; Accountants & Taxes, Journal. In the From field, type the appropriate from and to dates.

2. Select Customize Reort. The Modify Report: Journal window appears. Select the Filters tab.

3. In the Filter list, select Transaction Type. In the Transaction Type field, select Bill Payment.

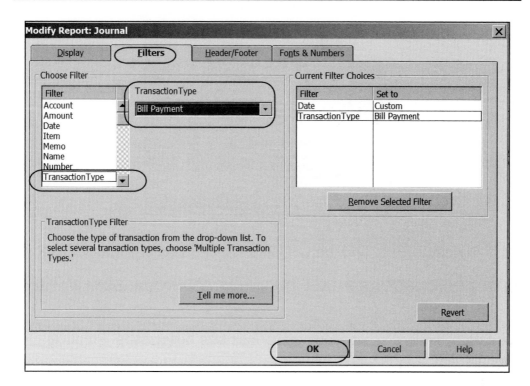

4. Click <OK>. The Journal appears with the vendor payments (Bill Pmt-Check) shown.

TOGGLE QUICKBOOKS TO ANOTHER VERSION

The student trial version software, included with *Computer Accounting Essentials with QuickBooks 2012*, can be used on one computer for 140 days.

Before following these steps, check with your instructor for his or her preference. The software site license purchased by the school and the 140-day CD included with *Computer Accounting Essentials with QuickBooks 2012* are the same software version.

1. From the menu bar, select File; Toggle to Another Edition. The Select QuickBooks Industry-Specific Edition window appears. In this example, QuickBooks Pro is selected.

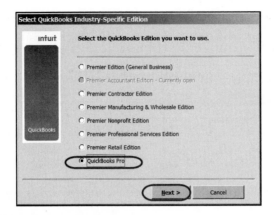

2. Click [**Next >**] and the version of QuickBooks changes to the Pro.

INTUIT QUICKBOOKS SMALL BUSINESS FINANCIAL SOFTWARE

QuickBooks offers applications for various size businesses. Products include:

1. QuickBooks Online
2. QuickBooks Pro 2012
3. QuickBooks Premier 2012
4. QuickBooks Accountant 2012
5. QuickBooks Enterprise Solutions

To learn more, go online to
http://proadvisor.intuit.com/commerce/catalog/fragments/quickbooks_products.jsp

UNINSTALL QUICKBOOKS AND REMOVE ALL QUICKBOOKS FILES AND FOLDERS

If you want to completely remove QuickBooks and remove QuickBooks installation files and folders left behind by Microsoft Add or Remove Programs utility, go online to this article for instructions http://support.intuit.co.uk/quickbooks/en-gb/kb/install-and-setup/install-quickbooks/1368.html?printIt=1. Windows Vista/7 instructions follow.

Important: A "clean uninstall" requires all other Intuit software applications that share the same installation folder to be reinstalled. If you need to preserve your old QuickBooks installation folders and file names, refer to the article Install

QuickBooks in a new folder for troubleshooting and resolving issues. http://support.quickbooks.intuit.com/support/Articles/HOW12273.

Back up your company file to a safe location to prevent it from being deleted or overwritten.

Have your QuickBooks installation CD-ROM and product numbers handy before reinstalling QuickBooks.

Perform a clean uninstall:

1. Click the Start button and then Control Panel.
2. In Windows 7/Vista, select Programs and Features. (In XP Select Add/Remove Programs.
3. Select Uninstall. (In XP select QuickBooks and click Change or Remove Programs).
   If necessary, repeat steps 1 through 3 to uninstall the QuickBooks Product Listing service.
4. Close Control Panel.

The clean uninstall procedure requires manually removing or renaming some QuickBooks installation folders.

Removing Intuit Folder

Removing the entire Intuit folder removes all subfolders that are contained within it.
If you do <u>not</u> have other Intuit products installed on your computer (such as Quicken, QuickTax, ProFile, other versions of QuickBooks, etc.) remove the Intuit folders listed below.

Windows 7/Vista

- C:\ProgramData\Intuit
- C:\ProgramData\Common Files\Intuit
- C:\Users\<current user>\AppData\Local\Intuit
- C:\Users\Public\Public Documents\Intuit
- C:\Program Files (x86)\Intuit (On Vista or XP, Program Files)

- C:\Program Files (x86)\Common Files\Intuit
- C:\Porgram Files\Common\Intuit
- Look in your Documents folder. If an Intuit folder exists, delete it. On Windows 7 computers, the Documents folder is in Libraries.

After removing the Intuit folders, empty the recycle bin.

Once QuickBooks is completely removed from your system, you may proceed with a new installation.

Appendix C

Glossary

Appendix C lists a glossary of terms used in *Computer Accounting Essentials with QuickBooks 2012, 6th Edition*. Appendix C is also included on the textbook website at www.mhhe.com/QBessentials2012, link to Student Edition, then select Glossary.

accounting equation
The accounting equation is stated as assets = liabilities + equities. (p. 245)

accounts payable
A group of accounts that show the amounts owed to vendors or credits for goods, supplies, or services purchased on account. (p. 110)

accounts payable transactions
Purchases on account from vendors. (p. 110)

accounts receivable
Group of accounts that show the amounts customers owe for services or products sold on credit. (p. 134)

accounts receivable ledger
Customers and receivables accounts which are grouped together. (p. 140)

accounts receivable transactions
Credit transactions from customers. (p. 134)

account reconciliation	As you write checks, withdraw money, make deposits, and incur bank charges, each of these transactions is recorded in QuickBooks and then "matched" with the bank's records. This matching process is called reconciliation. (p. 88)
assets	The organization's resources that have future or potential value. (p. 245)
backing up	Saving your data to a hard drive, network drive, or external media. Backing up insures that you can start where you left off the last time you used QB 2012. (p. 30)
balance sheet	Lists the types and amounts of assets, liabilities, and equity as of a specific date. (p. 73)
chart of accounts	List of all the accounts in the company's general ledger. (p. 67)
closing the fiscal year	Moving expense and revenue accounts to retained earnings. (p. 189)
compound transaction	An entry that affects three or more accounts. (p. 174)
content pane	Displays information about the company. For example, when the Home button is selected, the workflow diagrams for Vendors, Customers, Employees, Company, and Banking are shown. (p. 39)

credit sales	Refers to sales made to customers that will be paid for later. (p. 140)
customer invoice	Request for payment to a customer for products or services sold. (p. 134)
desktop	Also called content pane, desktop, or Home page. (p. 39)
equities	The difference between the company's assets and liabilities. (p. 245)
external media	Backing up to a drive other than the computer's hard drive or network drive. (p. 18)
general journal entries	The general journal shows the debits and credits of transactions and can be used to record any type of transaction. In this text, you use the general journal to record adjusting and closing entries. (p. 174)
graphical user interface (GUI)	The general look of a program is called its graphical user interface. (p. 37)
home page	Displays information about the company. The QB Home page includes areas for vendors, customers, employees, company, banking and their accompanying workflow processes. (p. 39)

income statement	An income statement is where a business reports its revenues and expenses and determines its net income or loss for a period. QuickBooks refers to the income statements as the Profit & Loss Statement. (p. 186)
icon bar	The icon bar shows pictures of common tasks, for example, the Home button shows a house, Calendar button shows a date, etc. The icon bar is also called the Navigation Bar. (p. 37)
inventory items	A product that is purchased for sale and is tracked in the Inventory account on the balance sheet. (p. 115)
liabilities	Liabilities are the company's responsibilities to others. Liability accounts include accounts payable, notes payable, unearned rent, etc. (p. 245)
menu bar	Contains menus for File, Edit, View, Lists, Company, Customers, Vendors, Employees, Banking, Reports, Online Services, Window and Help. (p. 38)
navigation bar	QB 2012 includes a graphical alternative to the menu bar. The Navigation Bar contains quick links to Home, Calendar, Snapshots, Customers, Vendors, Employees, etc. (p. 39)

profit & loss statement	This report is also known as an income statement. It summarizes income and expenses for the month, so you can tell whether you're operating at a profit or a loss. The report shows subtotals for each income or expense account in your chart of accounts. The last line shows your net income (or loss) for the month. (p. 186)
resourceful QuickBooks	On the QB menu bar, select Help, Learning Center Tutorials to watch the following types of videos: overview and setup, customers and sales, vendors and expenses, inventory, payroll, process payments, what's new. (pp. 22, 58, 102, 167, 194, 213)
restore	Previously backed up data can be restored or retrieved from the File menu's Restore Previous Local Backup selection. Files can also be restored from the No Company Open window; select the Open or restore an existing company. (p. 18)
statement of financial position	Lists the types and amounts of assets, liabilities, and equity as of a specific date. Also called the balance sheet. (p. 73)
taskbar	In Windows 7/Vista/XP, the Start button and taskbar are located at the bottom of the screen. (p. 39)
title bar	Contains company name and the program name. (p. 38)

trial balance	A report that adds up all the debits and credits. (p. 97)
USB drive	USB is an abbreviation of Universal Serial Bus. USB drives are known as flash drives, pen drives, etc. USBs are used as storage media. (p. 2)
vendors	A person or company from which the company buys products or services. (p. 110)

Index